REGIONAL MUSEUMS
IN NORTHERN IRELAND

First published 1978

ISBN   0 337 04092 3

A. C. Brooke Esq.,
Permanent Secretary,
Department of Education for Northern Ireland.

11 May, 1978.

Dear Mr. Brooke,

I have pleasure in presenting the Report of the Working Party on Regional Museums. The Party's first meeting was on 29 June 1977, so we have completed our work within the year. This satisfactory result is due to the enthusiasm shown by all the members and their preparedness to spend long days in furthering the work, often at personal inconvenience and in spite of travel problems. For this I am grateful to them.

Our Report recommends for your consideration both a museum structure and a regional museum service. In arriving at these conclusions we may have placed a somewhat liberal interpretation on our remit but we could not do otherwise if we were to examine all the considerations.

We have in the course of our task reviewed the resources of the province and have received much assistance in so doing from the various Government Departments and other organisations who have submitted their views to us orally and in writing. We have discussed many of these in our Report and have often quoted from their submissions. Not all, however, could be separately mentioned, so I take this opportunity to thank them for their help. They will almost all find some reference in the Report which they may look upon as an echo of their opinions.

Indeed if there is any one point which I should mention specially, it would be to underline the unanimity of purpose of those who submitted evidence to us. There is of course room for difference of detail but it is very noteworthy that the recommendations we have made will in my view go a very long way to satisfying the expressed views of the interested parties. Furthermore we consider that the implementation of our recommendations would greatly enhance the quality of life for the people of Northern Ireland.

We understand the difficulties of financing a policy such as we recommend and I have been at pains to ensure that there are no misapprehensions about the financial situation. It is fully appreciated that the implementation of any departmental policy as a result of this Report will have to await the provision of funds by Parliament, whenever that may be possible.

Finally I should like to express the gratitude of the Working Party to your Department for the most excellent support given to us in all our work and in the preparation and publication of this Report. I must mention particularly the enthusiasm and efficiency of Mr. B. S. Morrow who as our Secretary has managed our affairs and recorded our proceedings in a most able and competent way, and without whose devotion to duty we certainly could not possibly have completed our Report so speedily.

Yours sincerely,

W. G. MALCOLM,
Chairman.

v

ACKNOWLEDGEMENTS

We are grateful to the Ulster Museum for assistance in the design of the cover and to Mr. G. Burns for assistance in the preparation of the map. For permission to reproduce photographs we are grateful to the Director of the Arts Council of Northern Ireland (plate 11), the Department of Agriculture (plate 4), the Curator of the Fermanagh County Museum (plate 7), the Director of the Ulster Folk and Transport Museum (plates 2, 3 and 9), and the Director of the Ulster Museum (plates 1, 5, 6, 8 and 10). We are grateful also to those bodies which supplied attendance figures for their institutions for inclusion in the Report.

TABLE OF CONTENTS

LIST OF PLATES

I. INTRODUCTION

1. The Working Party was established by the Department of Education in May 1977. Our terms of reference were:

"to examine and make recommendations in relation to the development of regional or local museums in Northern Ireland."

2. The members of the Working Party were:

Mr. W. G. Malcolm, C.B., M.B.E., M.A.	—Chairman
Mr. G. Burns, B.Sc. (Econ.)	—Association of Local Authorities of Northern Ireland
Mr. R. R. Johnston, B.A.	—Department of Education
Professor F. J. Lelièvre, M.A., F.C.P.	—Association of Northern Ireland Education and Library Boards
Dr. W. A. McCutcheon, M.A.. F.S.A., F.R.G.S.	—Director, Ulster Museum
Mr. G. B. Thompson, O.B.E., M.Sc., F.M.A.	—Director, Ulster Folk and Transport Museum
Secretary	
Mr. B. S. Morrow, B.A.	—Department of Education

3. Mr. W. R. H. Carson, F.L.A., represented the Association of Education and Library Boards at the first meeting of the Working Party, prior to the appointment of Professor Lelièvre by the Association as its substantive representative. We are grateful to him for his contribution.

4. The Working Party had its first meeting on 29 June 1977. We held 13 full meetings in all, the last on 11 April 1978. We also paid a number of visits, as indicated later.

5. The subject we were asked to investigate—museum development at regional or local level—has aroused considerable interest over recent years in both Great Britain and Northern Ireland. In 1972, in line with developments elsewhere in the United Kingdom, the Ulster Museum considered the subject, and a policy document was prepared by the then Director, Mr. Alan Warhurst,* and his staff, and was subsequently adopted by the Museum's Trustees. This document, as revised in 1975, recommended that a regional museum service should be established, operated by the Ulster Museum in co-operation with the Ulster Folk and Transport Museum. Where appropriate the aid of other centralised bodies such as the Arts Council, the National Trust, and the Public Record Office would be enlisted, together with local societies and organisations with a good record of serious field work.

---

* Now Director of the Manchester Museum.

6. The service was seen as having six aims:

a. education: to give the people of Northern Ireland residing outside Belfast an opportunity to see and enjoy museum material illustrating the history and natural history of their area.

b. collecting: to encourage the proper collection and collation of objects and information in areas of the province which might be more easily encouraged to channel such material through a local centre rather than to a single centre in Belfast.

c. conservation: to ensure that objects of importance, e.g. paintings, antiquities, are properly conserved whether in museum ownership, " in situ " in the field, or even in private ownership subject to satis-factory negotiations.

d. research: to provide " consulting " facilities between local people and the staff of the national museums (i.e. Ulster Museum and Ulster Folk and Transport Museum) for the exchange of information which would improve our understanding of the scientific, historical and cultural environment of the area.

e. exhibitions: to provide temporary exhibitions of material such as travelling exhibitions from the Victoria and Albert Museum or the Science Museum, which would not normally be seen by people outside Belfast.

f. ancillary services: in addition a good many other important functions could be fulfilled, e.g. the provision of a lecture service both for schools and adults, an enquiry service, an identification service, various educational services.

7. A three tier museum structure was envisaged for the province, consisting of:

a. the Ulster Museum and the Ulster Folk and Transport Museum;

b. five or six regional museum centres;

c. a fluid third tier of museums or related institutions, geared to the second tier, which might in certain circumstances receive support from the regional service.

8. The Ulster Museum document did not come before the Department of Education* for formal approval as policy, but discussions have taken place about museum developments over the last few years between the Ulster Museum and individual district councils. A limited number of council developments, of varying scope and scale of operation, have gone forward, and additional developments are currently at various stages of planning or consideration by other councils. A number of museum or museum-type developments have also taken place as a result of private initiative.

* Hereafter for convenience referred to as the Department.

2

9. The ideas put forward in the Ulster Museum document—and the substantial interest which exists throughout the the province in museum development at a regional or local level—have raised a number of important questions of policy. This led to the establishment of the Working Party. The Department, however, made it clear that finance was unlikely to be available for regional or local museum development for several years ahead and in our deliberations we were careful to bear this point in mind.

II. HOW WE WORKED

10. We began by writing to Government Departments, seeking their views and asking them to let us know of any bodies for which they were responsible, directly or indirectly, which they thought we might wish to contact. All Departments suggested bodies for possible consultation, and whilst most Departments did not submit evidence to the Working Party themselves, the Departments of Agriculture, Commerce, and the Environment identified areas of common interest with the Working Party—in relation to state forests, tourist developments, and planning, country parks and other natural amenities respectively. We subsequently had the benefit of discussions with representatives of these Departments on these subjects. We also visited two forest parks and a country park to see developments there and we are grateful to the Departments of Agriculture and the Environment for their help.

11. Following our initial contact with Government Departments we wrote to a wide range of bodies and individuals, seeking their views on museum development at regional and local level, with particular reference to:

    a. the need for regional museums and/or a regional museum service;

    b. the functions and aims of regional museums and/or a museum service;

    c. organisation and funding;

    d. the relationship of regional museums and/or a museum service with:

        i. existing provision at a national (i.e. provincial) and local level;

        ii. interested local bodies;

    e. the use which the evidencing body might make of the service and the contribution it might make to it.

12. At the same time submissions were commissioned from Mr. Burns and Professor Lelièvre on behalf of their respective Associations, and from Dr. McCutcheon and Mr. Thompson on behalf of their respective Museums.

13. Evidence was received from 50 bodies and individuals in all, and these are listed in Appendix A.

14. The Working Party devoted much time to the consideration of these submissions, and in certain cases it sought supplementary evidence. Representatives from 11 bodies provided supplementary, oral, evidence and these bodies are listed in Appendix B.

15. An important part of our work consisted of seeking to acquaint ourselves with the variety of museum provision which currently exists in Northern Ireland, with current proposals for future developments, and with

the problems associated with museum development generally. In furtherance of this we made seven visits (including those mentioned at paragraph 10 above) to centres throughout the province, and in the course of these we saw a number of establishments, both unique and typical, and of varied scope and scale of operation. The visits also gave us an opportunity to learn of the needs of these establishments, and in some cases of plans for future developments. We are grateful to the authorities concerned for receiving us on these visits.

16. We also consulted published reports and documents, some of which are quoted from and acknowledged in the body of our Report. Apart from those we should also mention the recently published Report of the Resources Panel of the Northern Ireland Council for Continuing Education* and the Feasibility Study on the Organization of Educational Technology in Northern Ireland carried out by Mr. C. R. Latchem on behalf of the Council for Educational Technology for the United Kingdom.† There is some common ground between our work and the areas covered by these two Reports and their content has been of assistance to us. Our conclusions in those areas of common interest do not materially differ from theirs.

17. Expert advice was also sought on occasion on matters of a specialist nature, and the assistance given to us is acknowledged in the appropriate sections of the Report.

* HMSO, 1977.

† Council for Educational Technology for the United Kingdom, 1977.

III. REVIEW OF EXISTING RESOURCES

18. Where the museum scene is concerned the past two decades have been a period of remarkable development, not only in terms of physical expansion but also in the extent to which the interest and support of both central and local government have been applied to basic issues of administration and finance. Of particular note is the fact that between 1958 and 1967 no fewer than four Acts of Parliament concerned with museum development and reorganisation were passed at Stormont. These were subsequently added to by the Museums (Northern Ireland) Order, 1973, which extended still further a comprehensive programme of growth and rationalisation.

19. Merely to see the past twenty years as a belated if welcome recognition of the social importance of museums within a community would, however, be doing the province a disservice, for it could be claimed with considerable justification that museum development—or at least the interests and activities which engendered it—has long been a significant feature of Ulster life. What more impressive example could one cite than the fact that the establishment in 1759 of the British Museum itself originated with the collections of Dr. Hans Sloane of Killyleagh, Co. Down? Perhaps the passage of time has also clouded to some extent the origins of the Ulster Museum (formerly the Belfast Museum and Art Gallery) in the collections and activities of the Belfast Natural History and Philosophical Society, a distinguished local learned society founded in 1821. Its formation could be seen as a response to a need felt by a number of Ulster individuals from various walks of life for a means of focussing their interests, notably in the several branches of natural history and in antiquities. The same spirit of scientific enquiry had already given us the Armagh Observatory, founded in 1791.

20. Ulster of the 18th and 19th centuries was thus not lacking in men of intellect and collecting instincts, curious to know more of the world of nature and of man both at home and abroad. Not only were their endeavours locally based; some travelled abroad and enriched the Society's collections with artefacts from the far corners of the earth, whilst others working at home developed reputations which travelled abroad. One thinks, for example, of the Rev. Edward Hincks—a Church of Ireland Rector of Killyleagh of a somewhat retiring nature—who was acknowledged as one of the pioneers of Egyptology, and indeed in 1906 a marble bust was placed in his honour in the entrance hall of Cairo Museum.

21. Today our museums are developing on a scale worthy of the long tradition of scholarship from which they emerged. The museum instinct is as active today as in the past not only among those professionally involved in museum work, but also among the general public. Recent developments, impressive in themselves, have nevertheless indicated areas and directions

in which further development could desirably take place. Since Belfast and its immediate hinterland are now well endowed with museum facilities, the next logical consideration is the extension of museum services throughout the province.

22.   One of our first tasks in consequence was to review the existing museum resources of the province. This review is set out below and, while not exhaustive, it ranges widely so as to cover not merely places which come within the conventional understanding of " museum " but every facility which can be usefully included. This accords with the broad definition of museum which we have adopted in Section IV—paragraphs 85 and 86 below.

23.   Northern Ireland has two national museums—the Ulster Museum and the Ulster Folk and Transport Museum—both of which are financed by government grant through the Department of Education.

24.   As mentioned above the ULSTER MUSEUM evolved from the former Belfast Museum and Art Gallery by virtue of the Museum Act (Northern Ireland) 1961. The Belfast Museum and Art Gallery could in turn trace its roots as far back as 1821, to the formation of the Belfast Natural History Society.

25.   The Museum is situated in the Botanic Gardens, Stranmillis, Belfast. The first section of this building was opened in 1929 and a large extension was completed in 1972. The Museum has five academic Departments—Antiquities, Art, Botany and Zoology, Geology, and Technology and Local History, with Numismatics—as well as Departments of Design and Production, and Education. These last two Departments have responsibility, respectively, for the various aspects of display and interpretation, and in catering for the rapidly growing demand for educational facilities and resource utilisation.

26.   The Department of Antiquities is primarily concerned with the collection and preservation of the Irish archaeological material of all periods from the first arrival of man in Ireland prior to 6,000 B.C. to the end of the 17th century. The collections are notable for Irish Mesolithic flint implements, Neolithic flint, stone and pottery, Bronze Age gold and a particularly fine series of Early Iron Age bronze artwork. Later Iron Age and Medieval antiquities include some large and important groups of recently excavated material. In addition the Department maintains collections of non-Irish antiquities and ethnographic material for comparative purposes.

27.   The collections held by the Department of Antiquities have been greatly enhanced by the acquisition of the Girona Treasure, a collection of gold and silver coins, jewellery and objects of everyday use, recovered by Robert Stenuit, the Belgian underwater archaeologist, during 1967-69, from the site of the shipwreck of the Spanish Armada galleass *Girona*, off the North Antrim coast. This remarkable group of objects is on public exhibition, displayed with information about the circumstances of the wreck and its subsequent recovery.

28.   The Department of Art is particularly rich in Irish painting and possesses a number of Continental masters of the 17th and early 18th centuries, as well as early British and Irish watercolours. An important collection of contemporary art has been built up through the years. There are fine collections of Irish silver, glassware and furniture.

29.   The Department of Botany and Zoology collects examples of animals and plants found in Ireland. Research is an essential part of the Department's work and members of staff are associated with national and international projects. The collections, which are large, have been built up over almost two centuries and cover the main groups of plants and animals of Ireland, with comparative material from elsewhere. The aim of the Department is to encourage the public to appreciate and preserve the wildlife of Ireland. The present Natural Sciences galleries (see plate 1) were opened in September 1973 and a further display, dealing with marine life, is currently being set up.

30.   The Department of Geology houses an important and rapidly growing collection of Irish geological material, including rocks, minerals and fossils. The services of the Department are geared to all levels of interest, from the casual enquirer to the specialist geologist wishing to conduct research. The displays which opened in 1972 show undersea scenes of over 300 million years ago, river systems and deltas being formed, volcanoes erupting, minerals which glow in the dark, part of the expanding gemstone collection and many other treasures. A new three-dimensional geological display has been opened recently.

31.   The Department of Technology and Local History comprises five galleries. These cover power technology, flax and linen technology, local industries and crafts, local history, and numismatics. In the spacious Engineering Hall the exhibits on power technology include a large vertical waterwheel, a horizontal waterwheel, an impulse turbine and three large steam engines, with an overall emphasis on size and movement. The Textile Gallery contains a wide-ranging selection of flax and linen machinery. Both displays are backed up by detailed graphics of a new and exciting nature. The gallery which will be devoted to miscellaneous local industries and crafts is not yet open to the public but will include displays on domestic linen manufacture, rope making, ship building and horology. The new displays on local history illustrate the general political, social and military history of the province from the 17th century up to the present day and the numismatic cabinet, which contains some 40,000 specimens, is one of the major international collections.

32.   The Museum also holds numerous exhibitions illustrating special themes or points of topical interest and receives frequent travelling and loan exhibitions from other museums or related cultural organisations. Facilities are available for recognised research workers to make use of the extensive study collections. An Education Officer is available to advise teachers on how the Museum and its collections may be used to the best advantage and there is an expanding educational service catering for a wide range of interests and needs. There is a regular winter programme of public lectures,

films, and concerts, and special Saturday film shows for children. The Museum's lecture theatre, which has recently been refurbished, can seat 180 and has an extensive range of modern equipment.

33. The Museum has 147 full-time and 32 part-time staff. These figures include staff of the Armagh County Museum—see paragraphs 49 and 50 below. It is managed by a Board of 14 Trustees, 9 of whom are appointed by the Minister of Education, 1 by The Queen's University of Belfast, 1 by The New University of Ulster, and 3 by Belfast City Council.

34. Recurrent expenditure on the Museum amounted to £802,000 in 1976/77, and £872,000 in 1977/78. In addition the Museum has received in each of these years a purchase grant of £90,000. These figures include expenditure on the Armagh County Museum—see paragraphs 49 and 50 below.

35. Attendance figures for the Ulster Museum (excluding the Armagh County Museum) from 1972-1977 may be found in Appendix C1.

Plate 1—In the Natural Sciences galleries at the Ulster Museum

Plate 2—A waterwheel being placed in position during the reconstruction of the spade mill at the Ulster Folk and Transport Museum

36. The other national museum—The ULSTER FOLK AND TRANS-PORT MUSEUM—was established as the Ulster Folk Museum directly by legislation, under the Ulster Folk Museum Act (Northern Ireland) 1958. A 136 acre site at Cultra was acquired in 1961 and the Museum was officially opened to the public in 1964. At first it operated solely as a Folk Museum but in 1967 it was merged with the Belfast Transport Museum at Witham Street which had been in operation for some years under the Belfast Corporation and displayed a large and varied range of historic vehicles. An additional 40 acres of land were purchased at Cultra as the site for a more expansive Transport Museum and the first group of new galleries was opened in 1976. At present it houses part of the collection; the rest will remain open to the public at Witham Street until additional accommodation at Cultra becomes available. In 1973 the institution was renamed the Ulster Folk and Transport Museum.

37. The folk element of the Museum consists of an outdoor folk park at the centre of which is an Edwardian mansion, Cultra Manor, which, for the time being, houses the Museum's administrative headquarters and a limited number of galleries containing a range of folk exhibits from the general collection. These galleries will be replaced in time by new and more spacious accommodation elsewhere in the estate. In the folk park, which is still in the course of development, the aim is to reconstruct a representative

series of original buildings as they were within the past two hundred years. The buildings not only illustrate varied aspects and levels of Ulster life but are being arranged so as to show significant local settlement patterns. The first reconstructed house—an 18th century labourer's cottage from Co. Londonderry—was opened to the public in 1963. Since then further transplanted buildings have been opened regularly and to date the range comprises a 19th century water-powered spade mill and finishing shops from Co. Tyrone (see plate 2); the dwelling and out-buildings of a Co. Antrim hill-farm, rebuilt in the form it had assumed by the early 1900s; a mud-built facsimile of an 18th century linen weaver's house from Co. Down; a 19th century water-powered scutch mill from Co. Tyrone; a late 18th century bleachgreen watch hut from Co. Down; a hipped-roof farmhouse, of the same date, from Florence Court, Co. Fermanagh; a 19th century blacksmith's forge from Co. Fermanagh; a two-storey early 18th century planter's farmhouse from Co. Antrim; an 18th century bedroom-over-byre type house from west Co. Tyrone, in company with a single-roomed late 19th century outshot-bed house from the same neighbourhood; a small two-storey national school dated 1836 from north Co. Antrim; a 19th century byre-dwelling from northwest Co. Donegal; and to complete the series so far, a terrace of six early 19th century industrial houses from Belfast. In the weaver's house the traditional craft of handloom weaving may be seen in operation.

38. The Museum's building staff is currently reconstructing the old parish church from Kilmore, Co. Down (which dates from 1792), and in the summer of 1978 will dismantle and remove to the folk park a small national school, dated 1865, from Banbridge, Co. Down, and a terrace of four 19th century industrial houses from Dromore, Co. Down.

39. The new galleries in the transport section of the Museum, which opened in May 1976, have a limited range of vehicles on display at present (see plate 3) but further galleries will eventually accommodate locomotives

Plate 3—Veteran cars on display in the new transport galleries at the Ulster Folk and Transport Museum

and rolling stock illustrative of Irish broad and narrow gauge railways, together with various specimens of tramcars once used in Belfast and in smaller light rail systems in other parts of the province (e.g. Giant's Causeway/ Portrush). Commercial road vehicles on display will include trolley and motor buses, fire and ambulance appliances, lorries, steam rollers and traction engines. There are also veteran and vintage motor cars and a selection of horse-drawn vehicles. In addition, it is intended that the developed Museum will feature water and air transport and several examples of small boats and light aircraft already in the Museum's possession comprise a nucleus for further expansion in these areas.

40. The Museum is still in the process of development. Stores and work-shops have recently been built and maintenance depots are nearing completion. Other development works are planned.

41. The Museum is also as much concerned with non-material as with material culture and a small specialist research staff is engaged on the study of dialect, oral tradition, folk music, custom, belief, etc., from which archives of documents and tape-recordings are being assembled. There is, too, a reference library already comprising some 20,000 volumes relating to local social history, Irish and comparative ethnology, transport history, etc.

42. The Museum regards its education role as of primary importance. An Education Department is developing its work in relation both to educational establishments at all levels and to the general public (see, for example, plate 9, page 56). Day courses have been mounted to acquaint teachers with the nature and availability of the Museum's resources for school project work. Since January 1978 the Museum has begun to take part in a scheme whereby a limited number of teachers are seconded to it for a term to enable them to gain detailed knowledge of its resources and their deployment. The Museum's transport building includes a multi-purpose gallery for use as a lecture hall, exhibition hall, etc.

43. The Museum employs 169 full-time and 16 part-time staff. It is managed by a Board of 15 Trustees, 7 of whom are appointed by the Minister of Education, 1 by The Queen's University of Belfast, 1 by The New University of Ulster, 2 by Belfast City Council, and 4 by the Association of Local Authorities of Northern Ireland representing District Councils.

44. Recurrent expenditure on the Museum amounted to £481,500 for 1976/77 and was £543,000 in 1977/78. In addition the Museum has received in each of these years a purchase grant of £10,000.

45. Attendance figures for the Museum from 1972-1977 may be found in Appendix C2.

46. ARMAGH COUNTY MUSEUM, which at present is our only developed example of a regional museum, is situated in the Mall, Armagh, in premises rented from the Armagh Natural History and Philosophical Society (see plate 6, page 34). The original museum collection was that of the Society but when Armagh County Council acquired the collection in 1930, it decided that the Museum should be representative of the County and

modified the collection accordingly. Thus the present collection is representative of County Armagh and of the adjacent districts in Tyrone and Down, and contains material relating to this area's history from prehistoric times, comprising sections on social history (including militaria and costume), technical history (particularly that of the railways of the area), and natural history. The Museum also has a specialist section containing paintings by Irish artists.

47. In addition to the collection on permanent display the Museum frequently receives travelling exhibitions, mainly from the Ulster Museum and the Arts Council but also from local groups. The Museum also mounts its own exhibitions which it circulates to places such as schools, libraries and teachers' centres in the area of the Southern Education and Library Board and sometimes further afield. In this context we were pleased to note the close links between the Museum and the Board. The Museum has also exchanged exhibitions and information with the Monaghan County Museum and has supplied material for joint exhibitions.

48. The Museum places considerable emphasis on the educational aspects of museum work, both in relation to the general public and educational institutions. Students from schools, training colleges and universities are given assistance in their research and, apart from the collections on display and in reserve, there is a very good library, and a small workroom, available to students for research purposes. In addition to its links with the Board the Museum has built up links with individual schools and school parties come regularly to the Museum, sometimes even from beyond the Board's catchment area. The Curator gives talks to schools, historical associations, field clubs, women's organisations, young farmers' clubs, etc., as requested, and both school and adult parties are frequently conducted around the Museum.

49. In 1973, following the reorganisation of local government and the disappearance of the Armagh County Council, Armagh County Museum was transferred to the control of the Ulster Museum. Under this arrangement the County Museum has become part of the Ulster Museum, with access to the specialist facilities of that Museum and to the Museum's purchase fund. It retains its old title of " Armagh County Museum " and management decisions are largely in the hands of a County Museum Management Committee on which interests from the Museum's catchment area are represented. The membership of the Armagh County Museum Management Committee is as follows:—

8 members appointed by the Ulster Museum Trustees (to include persons closely associated with the Ulster Folk and Transport Museum or its activities);

3 members nominated by the Southern Education and Library Board; and

4 members, one each nominated by Armagh District Council, Craigavon District Council, Newry and Mourne District Council and the Armagh Natural History and Philosophical Society.

50.   At present the Museum has a full-time professional Curator, together with 4 other full-time and 2 part-time staff. Expenditure on the County Museum is included in the overall Ulster Museum budget. Recurrent expenditure on the County Museum, excluding the cost of central Ulster Museum services, amounted to some £26,000 in 1976/77 and was in the region of £29,000 in 1977/78.

51.   Attendance figures for the County Museum from 1972-1977 may be found in Appendix C3.

52.   FERMANAGH COUNTY MUSEUM is operated by Fermanagh District Council and is financed from the district rate. The museum is housed in part of the restored 16th century Keep of the Castle Barracks, Enniskillen, which had housed a varied collection promoted by the Fermanagh County Council prior to local government reorganisation in 1973. The other part of the Keep houses the Royal Inniskilling Fusiliers Regimental Museum.

53.   The aim of the County Museum is to provide a permanent collection representative of an area centred on Co. Fermanagh and the nucleus of a collection already exists. Collections of art works and reference material are also being built up. The Museum opened in April 1977, but only for temporary exhibitions and for limited periods. It will become fully operational in May 1978 when the first stage of its permanent display of antiquities will be opened.

54.   Since opening, the Museum has housed various Arts Council, Ulster Museum and Ulster Folk and Transport Museum exhibitions, and others initiated locally. Lectures have been held in the Museum and archaeological tours have been arranged in conjunction with the Ulster Museum. School parties visit the Museum and a limited education service is provided.

55.   The Museum is at present staffed by a professional Curator and an assistant. General work is carried out by the Council's Works Department. Responsibility for museum policy is exercised through the Council's Arts and Museum Committee, a standing committee of the Council.

56.   Attendance figures for the Museum in 1977—including figures for the Royal Inniskilling Fusiliers Regimental Museum—are contained in Appendix C4.

57.   There are four main REGIMENTAL MUSEUMS in Northern Ireland:

1.   The Combined Irish Cavalry Museum in Carrickfergus Castle.

2.   The Royal Inniskilling Fusiliers Regimental Museum in the Keep, Castle Barracks, Enniskillen.

3.   The Royal Irish Fusiliers Regimental Museum in the Sovereign's House, The Mall, Armagh.

4.   The Royal Ulster Rifles Museum, in the War Memorial Building, Waring Street, Belfast.

These museums house displays of regimental uniforms, medals, silver, trophies, photographs and other items related to regimental history.

58. As an example of the number of visitors received by a regimental museum attendance figures for the Royal Irish Fusiliers Regimental Museum from 1972-1977 are given in Appendix C5. For attendances at the Royal Inniskilling Fusiliers Regimental Museum see Appendix C4. At present the Royal Ulster Rifles Museum is not directly open to the public.

59. The ULSTER-AMERICAN FOLK PARK is situated at Camphill, near Omagh, Co. Tyrone. In complementary sections representing the Old World and the New it illustrates through a series of furnished buildings—both original reconstructions and accurate reproductions—the story of the emigrations of Ulster people to America in the 18th and 19th centuries and of the contribution they made to the USA throughout the whole period of its birth and development. There is an exhibition and information centre containing a lecture and film theatre and a permanent display employing modern audio-visual techniques. The Park opened in July 1976 and is still in the process of development. Numerous school parties have visited the Park, which has two Education Officers seconded on its staff to cater for school needs, as well as a curatorial officer and an administrative officer, all under a Chief Executive.

60. The Park is vested in the Scotch-Irish Trust of Ulster, which was set up in 1967 with the aid of an endowment provided by the Mellon family of Pittsburgh to restore the farmhouse home of their ancestor Judge Thomas Mellon at Camphill. The Park grew up around this and a number of its buildings, and the life styles presented in the Park, have associations with the Mellon family. The Mellon family provided funds for the construction of the exhibition and infomation centre and continues to be associated with the Park financially and otherwise.

61. The Park is financed largely out of government funds and financial control is exercised by the Central Secretariat and the Department of the Civil Service. There is an advisory management committee.

62. Attendance figures for the Park since it opened are contained in Appendix C6.

63. The NATIONAL TRUST preserves places of historic interest and natural beauty and it maintains over forty properties in all parts of Northern Ireland. These include the houses at Castle Ward, Co. Down, and Florence Court, Co. Fermanagh, the Rowallane Gardens, Saintfield, Co. Down, the Giant's Causeway, and some 10 miles of Causeway Coast, Co. Antrim, and

the Murlough Nature Reserve, Dundrum, Co. Down. The Trust has acted hitherto as agent for the Scotch-Irish Trust of Ulster in administering houses at Cullybackey, Co. Antrim, and Dergalt, Co. Tyrone, which have links with American Presidents, Chester A. Arthur and Woodrow Wilson respectively, but is in process of handing them over to the Scotch-Irish Trust. In some of the Trust's properties small museum-type collections have grown up in addition to the normal fittings and furnishings of the property. The costume collection at Springhill, Co. Londonderry, is an example.

64. An important area of the Trust's work is nature conservation and as an example of this for some years it has operated the Strangford Lough Wildlife Scheme aimed at conserving the amenities of the Lough. This covers 80% of the foreshore of Strangford Lough and includes measures for the protection of plant and fish life and for control of predators and litter. The Trust provides bird refuges and viewpoints, with hides and identification panels for visitors' use. Schools and study groups are encouraged to use the Lough as an outdoor classroom and together with local field groups are encouraged to participate in the Trust-operated schemes relating to the Lough. The Trust has recently opened an educational nature reserve created from worked-out clay pits at Glastry, near Kircubbin, Co. Down.

65. The Trust at present has no education officer but it has useful links with teachers' centres. In addition to producing literature on its properties for the general public, it is seeking to meet the needs of schools by the production of education packs. In addition, in conjunction with the national museums, the Public Record Office and the Ulster-American Folk Park, the Trust is currently engaged in preparing specimen case studies to show how teachers might make the best use of a property or local source.

66. The Trust is a charity dependent on membership subscriptions, entrance fees, legacies and endowments. It has on occasion received grants from the Ulster Land Fund to enable it to acquire and maintain certain of the more important properties which could not have been accepted without this aid, and it may of course apply for other government grants where these are relevant. The Trust's powers are exercised locally by its Committee for Northern Ireland.

67. Attendance figures for a number of the Trust's houses, and estimated attendance figures for some of its open space properties, are contained in Appendix C7.

68. The Department of Agriculture, Forest Service, is responsible for some sixty state FORESTS in Northern Ireland, all of which are open to the public. Six of these, with a concentration of points of interest or particular specialist features, have been developed as FOREST PARKS and provided with facilities to cater for large numbers of visitors. At most parks these facilities include information centres, with exhibitions relating to the natural features of the forest and the work of the Forest Service. Some parks cater for school children by providing educational facilities. Information is also provided for

visitors on a more modest scale at forest parks and a number of other forests by means of, e.g. outdoor information panels and nature trails. At two forests—Randalstown, Co. Antrim, and Seskinore, Co. Tyrone—there are specialist wildlife educational facilities (see plate 4).

69. The six forest parks are located at Castlewellan and Tollymore, Co. Down, Drum Manor and Gortin Glen, Co. Tyrone, Glenariff, Co. Antrim, and Gosford, Co. Armagh. Of these Drum Manor, Glenariff, Gortin Glen and Tollymore have information centres, and a centre is at present being established at Castlewellan. Forest parks are currently planned at another four forests and at one of these, Parkanaur, Co. Tyrone, the Department of Agriculture is planning to develop a Forest Service Museum.

70. Attendance figures for the forest parks from 1972 to 1977 are contained in Appendix C8.

71. The Department of Agriculture is also engaged in nature conservation work and as part of this some 15 National Forest Nature Reserves and 23 local Forest Nature Reserves have been declared. See paragraph 73 below.

72. The Department of the Environment possesses powers to protect the natural amenities of Northern Ireland and among these is the power to acquire land for COUNTRY PARKS. To date five country parks have been set up, at the Roe Valley and the Ness, both in Co. Londonderry, Crawfordsburn and Scrabo, both in Co. Down, and Castle Archdale, Co. Fermanagh. Of these the Ness, Scrabo and Castle Archdale sites are at an early stage of development. Further land has been acquired at The Birches, Annaghmore, Co. Armagh, and is to become the Peatlands Country Park. An information centre has been established at the Roe Valley park and further centres are proposed for other parks. The Department will also shortly open the Portandoo Countryside Centre at Portrush, Co. Antrim.

Plate 4—A school party at the display centre at Randalstown Forest, Co. Antrim

73. Among the Department's other powers are the powers to designate areas as being of outstanding natural beauty, or of scientific interest, and to establish nature reserves. It has also the power to designate areas of the countryside as National Parks. There are 8 designated Areas of Outstanding Natural Beauty in Northern Ireland and one of these—the Lagan Valley—is being developed as a Regional Park. Some 45 Areas of Scientific Interest have been designated and some 31 Nature Reserves declared, including the National Forest Nature Reserves referred to above (paragraph 71). No National Parks have been designated.

74. Attendance figures are not available for country parks but given their individual locations the parks are well used, particularly during the summer season.

75. The PLANETARIUM, which is situated in the grounds of the Armagh Observatory, was officially opened in 1968. It has a star theatre and star projector, a hall of astronomy, a lecture room and a public observatory with a large reflecting telescope. With the completion of the hall of astronomy and the public observatory in 1975 the Planetarium facilities became the most extensive in the British Isles for the use of astronomy in education and there is a continuing programme of educational activities. Thus while the Planetarium caters for the public and tourists generally much of its work is concerned with schools.

76. The Planetarium was built with a tourist development grant from government and contributions from the Armagh County and Urban District Councils. Funds for the addition of the hall of astronomy and the public observatory were also provided from central government and local authority sources. Since 1975, in recognition of the extensive educational service provided, the Planetarium came under the Department of Education. The Southern Education and Library Board, in whose area the Planetarium is situated, meets the running costs. The Planetarium is managed by a Committee of Management, with a majority appointed by the Governors of the Armagh Observatory and the remainder by the Area Board.

77. Attendance figures for the Planetarium from 1972 to 1977 are contained in Appendix C9.

78. The PUBLIC RECORD OFFICE of Northern Ireland, which is situated in Balmoral Avenue, Belfast, is responsible for the reception and safe-keeping of the records of the Courts of Justice, Government Departments, local authorities and other public bodies. It has some 500 million documents including private documents of historical interest. The Public Record Office has reference room facilities and a manuscript room available for use by the public, together with a multi-purpose area which can be used for exhibitions and lectures. Specialist staff are available to assist enquirers with historical research.

79. The Public Record Office has a vigorous educational policy and has established links with a wide range of bodies associated with education throughout the province. In particular it has close links with the library services of the five Education and Library Boards, which have photocopied a considerable amount of Public Record Office material as documentary source material for local studies in their areas. There are links with teachers' centres, where curricular material is being developed, and since 1975 the Department of Education has operated a scheme whereby teachers may apply for a secondment for a period to the Public Record Office in order to get to know the scope of its resources and learn how best to use them—see paragraph 42 above.

80. Public Record Office staff lecture to adult education classes on topics of historical interest and on methods of research into local history, and the Public Record Office produces a number of historical publications, including Education Facsimiles, on themes of interest to the student of Irish history. It has collaborated with the Ulster Museum and the Ulster Folk and Transport Museum on joint exhibitions and publications and it is currently engaged with both museums and with the National Trust in two joint educational field exercises.

81. The ARTS COUNCIL, in addition to providing a continuous exhibition programme in its gallery in the centre of Belfast, also organises exhibitions which travel throughout the province. An idea of the variety of subject matter and the places visited can be gained from the list of attendance figures for exhibitions from 1972 to 1977 in Appendix D. The Council's main source of income is an annual grant in aid from the Department.

82. The point has already been made that this review is not exhaustive. Inevitably a number of resources, public and private, will have been omitted. For example, there are collections of a specialist nature owned by institutions such as the Churches and the Universities. Libraries, public and private, may also contain material which is of relevance.

83. It is evident from this review that the province is fortunate in having two excellent museums of national status and quite a number of other institutions of widely differing and often highly specialised nature, but perforce of a narrower scope, as dictated by their nature or location. It is also evident that there has hitherto never been any serious attempt to assess the needs of Northern Ireland as a whole. Consideration has never been given to organising and supplementing existing resources in such a way as to create a comprehensive museum structure serving the entire population, with easy reach and access for all.

84. There is obviously a real need for such consideration by central agency. As we see it, our task is to draw up a shopping list of the province's museum needs. So we may find out what is needed, where it is needed, who should provide it and how an early start may be made to achieving it. Thus we aim

at formulating a policy capable of being adopted by government such as, when implemented, would provide a suitable museum structure. It is true that our terms of reference call for us to consider—" the development of regional or local museums "—but this has led us into studying the whole field including the resources and services offered by the national museums. Hence our interpretation of the remit to us has of necessity been wide and flexible, and the objectives we recommend are consequently all-embracing.

IV. DEFINITION OF "MUSEUM"

85. It is necessary to consider what is meant by " museum ". Some members of the public have tended to regard museums as dusty buildings, full of dull display cabinets housing miscellaneous collections of old things, and showing perhaps some lack of imagination and certainly some tiredness on the part of the museum authorities. Modern museums, however, do not come within this concept in any way. We consider it most important that any policies adopted by central government or by local authorities or any other museum-owning body should be firmly aimed at securing a complete effacement of any vestiges of this out-of-date notion. A visit to the two national museums will fully demonstrate the modern approach to choice and display of exhibits and is strongly recommended to all who may be involved in museum policy-making and are not already familiar with these establishments.

86. But apart from the approach and the modes of display adopted there is also a question of scope. The range of establishments already listed is wide and diverse and some of them obviously are not by any means covered by the conventional idea of " museum " yet it seems to us that they should all have a place within a comprehensive plan. Hence the word " museum " will have to be given for our purposes the widest possible definition. Various possibilities were discussed and the one which commended itself is the International Council of Museums' definition which has been incorporated in the Museums Association recommended Code of Practice for Museum Authorities. According to paragraph 2.1 thereof, a museum should be:

> " a non-profit making, permanent institution, in the service of society and of its development, and open to the public, which acquires, con-serves, researches, communicates and exhibits, for the purposes of study, education and enjoyment, material evidence of man and his environment ".*

This we found entirely satisfactory for our purposes, particularly when read with the following extract from the Code of Practice, in which the Inter-national Council of Museums recognises that the following comply with this definition:

> "a. conservation institutes, and exhibition galleries permanently maintained by libraries and archive centres;
>
> b. natural, archaeological and ethnographic monuments and sites and historical monuments and sites of a museum nature, for their acquisition, conservation and communication activities;

* In adopting the phrase " non-profit making " we do not suggest that unprofitability is in itself to be desired but that the functions of a museum can be distorted if the making of profit becomes a principle.

21

c. institutions displaying live specimens, such as botanic and zoological gardens, aquaria, vivaria, etc.;

d. nature reserves;

e. science centres and planetaria ".

In this Report the word " museum " should from this point be considered to have the full wide meaning ascribed to it in this paragraph.

V. AIMS AND OBJECTIVES OF MUSEUMS

87. But the formal words of a definition are not enough, however necessary they are for administrators and lawyers. Probably any report about museums is incomplete if it does not discuss aims and objectives and all that can be said may already have been said many times over. Yet if this Report is to be capable of standing on its own feet, it will have to detail aims and objectives at some length, even at the risk of repetition, in the hope that this will help to guide all involved in the subject.

88. What then are the aims ? A simple summary lies in three words: collection, communication, research. Those are implicit in the definition we have adopted but some elaboration seems advisable so as to leave no doubt as to what we have in mind. Hence we now list some detailed aims in a purely arbitrary order. Opinions must differ as to priority, and we would not be dogmatic as to whether our order is right. Perhaps it does not matter very much—it is the content of the aims as a whole which does matter:

    a. to gather together material suitable for the museum's collection by acquisition from known sources or other collections, or by donation, or by seeking and finding items not previously considered as museum specimens or simply not discovered;

    b. to collate such material so as to form cohesive collection units, thereby initiating and establishing the pattern of further collecting endeavour, building up complete subject displays, and facilitating relations with other museums as to interchange of duplicated items;

    c. to preserve for the present and for posterity material which will lose or has lost its usefulness for everyday life and which will therefore disappear unless taken into safe custody, as well as materials which for some other reason have acquired a scarcity value;

    d. to conserve materials from deterioration by use of skilled techniques so that their quality may not be lost;

    e. to display to advantage the collections so that visitors may see, appreciate and understand the subjects grouped in the museum as a consequence of the policy objectives of the management;

    f. to inform visitors about the present and past of their environment in such a way as to widen the horizons of their knowledge and experience;

    g. to educate in the widest sense all ages of visitors and especially perhaps children, for whom museum displays can be an invaluable supplement to the more formal teaching of the classroom;

    h. to store collection items not for the time being required for display purposes but which are considered worthy of preservation either for change of display or for loan purposes;

i. to record collected items so that ready access can be gained when needed, or that gaps requiring to be filled by acquisitions can be the more readily identified, and that in the future it may be possible to have a composite list of items in the various collections throughout the province;

j. to carry out research or to provide access for research on the stored items;

k. last, and certainly not least, to please, since a live museum will gratify the senses and the intellect of visitors so that they leave with curiosity aroused or with the satisfaction of a rewarding experience.

89. Such are in our view the detailed aims. For a more general statement of objectives, we cannot improve on the wording, which we now quote, of paragraphs 4.2 and 4.3 of the Department of Education and Science Report entitled " Provincial Museums and Galleries "* (a document which we have found to be of considerable interest):

" 4.2 Museums can capture and preserve the standards and values of civilisation, can demonstrate man's achievements in art and science, and his failures. The best of what is past may give an insight into what will be most valuable in the future. When standards are being questioned and the pace of change quickens, museums perform an essential role as a point of reference and a place where the values of the past and present may be preserved and reflected upon. They have a responsibility to acquire and safeguard evidence and records.

4.3 Man's place in nature and the constituents, history and origins of the natural world are subjects of increasing interest and concern in an urbanised and more leisured society. Museums are in a unique position to alleviate ignorance and to foster and satisfy interests ".

90. A word of caution is nonetheless appropriate. The resources of an area like Northern Ireland are obviously limited and so too is its museum potential. The Ulster Museum, excellent as it is, does not compete with the scale and variety of the British Museum or the Victoria and Albert Museum. It has a policy of reflecting the local scene to a large extent, even in those aspects of its display which have a general import; thus the heavy engineering exhibits are inherited mainly from local factories, and much of the archaeological material has an Ulster provenance. (Plate 5 shows industrial steam engines in the Engineering Hall at the Ulster Museum.)

91. The Ulster Folk and Transport Museum has a similar policy, in its case defined by statute. The Folk side of its work is therefore specifically designed to preserve material and information, including original buildings

* HMSO, 1973.

Plate 5—Industrial steam engines in the Engineering Hall at the Ulster Museum

illustrative of " the way of life, past and present, and the traditions of the people of Northern Ireland ".* The Transport section has a very substantial collection of exhibits illustrating Irish transport history, with particular reference to Northern Ireland.

92. The lesson we wish to get across here is that a Northern Ireland museum should be so organised that it has a strong bearing on the local scene, or, like the Folk Museum, is derived largely from it. It is true that very specialised establishments, such as the Armagh Planetarium, cannot do much to conform to this requirement, but even specialised botanical or zoological museums could relate at least a part of their exhibits to a study and display of local flora or fauna respectively, where geographical or climatological accidents can so easily produce regional differences of great interest. We see great merit in this and recommend that museum authorities should have amongst their major objectives a reflection of the local scene.

* The Ulster Folk Museum Act (Northern Ireland), 1958.

VI. SHORTCOMINGS OF THE EXISTING SITUATION

a. Imbalance

93. Having considered resources, definitions, and aims and objectives, we now turn to consider the Northern Ireland scene in the light of these thoughts. We can identify several important defects in our museum structure, if indeed it is fair to use the word structure where there has been so far no central authority and no guiding plan.

94. In the first place this lack has led directly to a state of imbalance both geographical and quantitative. The province as a whole is well catered for at national museum level by the Ulster Museum and the Ulster Folk and Transport Museum, but both of these are, quite rightly, located in the same area, the one in Belfast, the other just a few miles to the eastward. Here they are in the most densely populated part of the province and are most easily visited by the largest possible number of people, as well as being readily accessible to transport from all parts. They are also likely to attract to themselves the largest possible patronage by visitors and tourists. They are, however, in consequence least accessible to the population furthest away from Belfast, in the west and south of the province.

95. The needs of the population in rural areas should be catered for primarily by regional museums, but of such there is only one—the Armagh County Museum. We have visited this and think it is a model of its kind. We commend its management and curators for the forward-looking policy followed through the years, with the result that the population of the area has had access to well-organised regional museum facilities. The rest of the province has no regional museums, though we commend the initiative of the Fermanagh District Council on the progress it is making in Enniskillen, and the progressive intentions of some other local authorities.

96. The remainder of our existing resources has grown up in particular areas almost by chance—regimental museums because of depot towns, nature centres because of forests or the accident of attractive scenery, and so on. The result is that, whilst other types of facility are to be found here and there throughout the province, there is an unbalanced position as regards museums in the narrower sense. There is thus frequently an absence of local museum manifestation such as may begin to create a feeling of curiosity. (The map at Appendix E shows the spread of resources.)

97. A serious consequence of the imbalance is that whereas in Armagh the local scene is mirrored by the County Museum, and local interests, especially

the Natural History and Philosophical Society,* are in various ways focussed upon the Museum, the other identifiable regions within the province have no central focussing institution and much of the record of their origins and history is in danger of loss and oblivion through neglect.

b. No Museum Service

98.   Museums require considerable resources of expertise in fields such as graphics, photography and display techniques, as well as traditional trades such as joinery, in order to show their exhibits to the best advantage, as well as to create travelling exhibitions (which are discussed in paragraphs 235–241). The two national museums have technical staff in these categories but we are informed by them both that their staff are inadequate in numbers and that workshop premises are too small and cramped for their own purposes, never mind trying to cater for the needs of other institutions. We have seen this for ourselves at the Ulster Museum especially. Further, neither museum has any duty to provide a service. The staff of the national museums have nevertheless done their best within the obvious constraints to help and advise people concerned with founding or running museums. It is very clear to us, however, that any significant growth in museum resources has been inhibited in the past and could be misguided in the future unless an adequate service with all the necessary skill resources can be provided.

99.   We will return to the question of a regional museum service later (see paragraphs 167–191) but it is now sufficient to register the view that the absence of such a service has been one of the important shortcomings. It may be arguable on a chicken and egg basis whether museums or the creation of a museum service should come first but this would be an academic and unprofitable exercise. It suffices to identify a museum service as an element that must be included in a future structure.

c. Supply of Skilled Staff

100.   The national museums have so far succeeded fairly well in filling staff vacancies with suitable people but at times posts have had to remain vacant for long periods until the right person was found. They have also had to recruit staff without formal museum training and bring them up to the standard required to fill vacancies. This is not easy to do on an ad hoc basis. The supply of skilled experts is thus seen to be a recurrent if not a constant problem for them.

101.   If some new museums are founded in the near future, staff recruitment is going to be difficult. Dilution of the present staff could lead to deterioration of existing standards yet in the new museums we consider that skilled management at the level of curator and indeed below this level is a must right from the start. Professionalism will be at a premium.

* See paragraph 234 regarding the importance of local societies.

102.   We see a need therefore for a central policy to identify staff needs in terms of numbers and qualifications.   These needs should be linked to a career structure and an agreed system of pay and conditions so that suitable new personnel may be attracted to our museums either from other spheres of employment in Northern Ireland or else from outside the province.

d. No Government Policy

103.   These shortcomings may all be ascribed perhaps to a further basic shortcoming—the absence of any positive government policy towards regional museums and a regional museum service.   In saying this we stress that we have nothing but praise for the past initiatives by central government in Northern Ireland which have resulted in the two national museums and the present approach which is to encourage them as far as possible within the constraints of limited capital resources.   Nevertheless we have now reached the stage at which the need for an overall policy has become clear to us.

104.   This particular shortcoming is of course well known to government and indeed it is consciousness of it which led the Department of Education to set up this Working Party.   There has been pressure for some time for the adoption of a positive policy, particularly from the past Director of the Ulster Museum, Mr. Alan Warhurst, and from the present Directors of the two national museums.   Indeed our deliberations have been to a large extent influenced by the resultant paper tabled for our consideration by the Directors.

105.   We feel strongly that a positive forward-looking policy towards the creation of regional museums and a regional museum service must be adopted by central government, and we recommend accordingly.   Only thus can the considerable surge of interest in the subject manifested to us in so many ways (as discussed in paragraphs 108–119) be channelled and encouraged, and assistance provided wherever it is needed and may be best employed.

106.   We hope we do not stray too far from our remit if we make the point that we welcome the fact that museum policy is now firmly in the hands of the Department of Education.   We hope that it will stay there.   We mention particularly the benefits of the obvious close linkage with the general field of education.   We emphasise too that possibilities of close co-operation at area and local levels have been strongly urged upon us by the Education and Library Boards.

107.   We have just discussed what is meant to be not so much a complete list of shortcomings as a grouping of the major points which have to be met by policy decisions.   The question of unsatisfied demands from the community is the next major issue to which we move.

VII. WHAT IS THE DEMAND FOR A MUSEUM STRUCTURE?

108. The evidence provided by written submissions and backed up orally by witnesses showed virtually complete unanimity in favour of the provision of regional museums and a regional museum service. Some interested bodies showed a preference for one rather than the other—generally for good reasons springing from their own particular involvement—but little in the way of adverse comment was received. The attitude of these bodies can conveniently be considered in groups.

Local Authorities

109. The views favoured generally by local authorities were admirably voiced to us by one of our members, Mr. G. Burns, the Clerk to the Fermanagh District Council. These were supported by the members of two councils whom we were glad to be able to meet—the Fermanagh District Council and the Londonderry City Council. We also received written submissions from eight individual councils of whom several wish to promote their own museum enterprises.

110. It is very clear that amongst the councils there is a strong feeling in favour of the establishment of regional museums and that this field of endeavour is one where the powers of councils should be exercised. The following extract from a letter received by the Working Party from the Carrickfergus Borough Council is quoted as a typical example of the attitude of Councils:

" The Council indicated its support for the establishment of such museums which could supplement those already in existence or in the process of being set up in the various areas. The Council envisaged that local museums would have a permanent section housing local exhibits and also sufficient space to take from the centre source a module or modules on various subjects and topics depending on the space available.

The Council would hope that the establishment of a museum as outlined above would have a considerable educational impact on the area, and would bring exhibits to the people as opposed to people travelling considerable distances to see exhibits."

Education and Library Boards

111. The views of the boards were likewise admirably voiced to us by Professor F. J. Lelièvre as a member of the Working Party and as representative of the Association of Northern Ireland Education and Library Boards. There is active community of interest between the boards and

29

museums, the more so since " museums have in some instances developed an educational service as part of their work." The Association considered that boards, whilst not likely to be directly involved in setting up museums, would be anxious to give them co-operation and support, and the feeling was again that considerable expansion in regional resources was necessary.

112. It was further argued that such an expansion could get assistance from the boards by active participation in management, by contribution to specific projects or acquisitions and of course by arranging attendances for educational purposes. There is also the probability of material assistance in relation to the provision of accommodation for museums. This would arise from the policy of encouragement of multi-use school premises, from possible redundant school buildings and from the obvious potential of libraries as exhibition areas. On the library side the boards' services include activities similar to some of those undertaken by museums and in certain fields, notably information storage and retrieval, they have experience and expertise to share.

Other Government Departments

113. The Departments of Agriculture, Commerce and the Environment all have interest in these problems since they are responsible for a variety of activities which may be covered by our definition of " museum ". These will be discussed later but at this stage it suffices to say that we have had assistance and advice from these departments and those bodies linked with them, and here also we find a general opinion in favour of expansion in regional museum resources.

Organisations

114. This heading covers nearly all the bodies listed in Appendix A as having submitted evidence to us, other than those just discussed in paragraphs 109 to 113. Some of these are already in the museum business in a big way throughout the province, for example:

The Historic Monuments Council cares for many places of great importance and interest, ranging from prehistoric stone circles to great medieval castles.

The National Trust has in its care or ownership such outstanding places as Castle Ward (which we visited) and the Giant's Causeway with the North Antrim Coastal Path (which nearly everyone has visited !).

The Arts Council has its frequent exhibitions, many of a travelling nature (which we have seen individually), and actively encourages all sorts of related artistic endeavour. It is particularly relevant to note that in recent years there has been an increasing liaison between the Council and the Ulster Museum in promoting and handling travelling exhibitions.

And so on—we need not continue to list the involvement of various bodies. But these examples lend force to the opinion we formed that throughout the committees, councils, and boards of directors of these bodies, i.e. the people most directly involved in the matters which concern us, there is a strong feeling that it is time Northern Ireland had an expanded museum structure as a result of a firm government policy.

The Directors of the two National Museums

115. Although they are both members of the Working Party, the two Directors have of course the right and indeed the duty to voice their own views and those of their Boards, being more closely involved than anyone else, and also their professional knowledge and experience must obviously count for a great deal. Their joint paper to the Working Party was the first basic document which we considered. It was a forthright recommendation of a three-tier structure, plus a regional service, and this is indeed roughly what we recommend in the following sections.

Public Demand

116. This is never an easy factor to assess, particularly when considering the provision of some facility hitherto missing from the picture. The views conveyed by the District Councils and, from a specialised point of view, the Education and Library Boards, gave us some indication of general feeling. The degree of patronage of existing museums is also a useful pointer and accordingly Appendix C gives attendance records at the two national museums and also at other museums where the governing bodies or curators have kindly assisted us by providing figures. The figures are of great interest and merit careful study.

117. We do, however, draw the conclusion that the statistics point to a very strong public interest in museums, all the more remarkable because of the adverse effects of the troubled times we live in and of the almost total absence of tourists and visitors from abroad. We are conscious indeed of the positive influence for good of museums (and the Arts in general) in the disturbed state of the province in recent years. We think it reasonable to conclude that expanded museum facilities will receive ample public support.

118. The growing public awareness of the environment we live in and what is now referred to as our natural heritage are also pointers to the attitude of the general public. The environment is continuously evolving and is changed and moulded by man's activities, sometimes for the good, only too often for the bad. The new and growing awareness of such matters brings with it hope that future changes may be less bad and that what is good—and in Northern Ireland there is so very much that is good—may be jealously guarded and conserved for our own present-day enjoyment and for the benefit of posterity. The link between this development of community attitudes and a forward-looking museum policy is obvious.

119. We feel that the active encouragement of museums in the broadest possible interpretation of our definition of the word is one of the most tangible ways of encouraging and harnessing the growing public awareness of the need to cherish and conserve what is best in our traditions and surroundings, and we so recommend.

31

VIII. A POSSIBLE THREE CATEGORY STRUCTURE

120. We have examined the shortcomings of the present provision of museums and we have considered opinions in favour of expansion. We conclude that a new structure is necessary and we recommend provision on the lines detailed in the following paragraphs.

121. Museums of all types, actual, in preparation, or planned, should be divided simply into three categories. The division is made partly for convenience of reference—since the category in which a museum would find itself would be some indication of its scope—and partly because different means of control and financial arrangements are indicated. These fall into three different approaches.

122. We recommend that the three categories of museum should be:

1. national museums;

2. regional museums;

3. display centres.

123. Throughout our discussions we have been talking from time to time of a " three-tier " museum arrangement as proposed to us by the paper submitted jointly by the Directors of the Ulster Museum and the Ulster Folk and Transport Museum. The expression " three-tier " has also become known to many of the persons and organisations who have submitted their views to us.

124. The expression does not, however, commend itself as one which we should try to pass into general usage through the medium of our Report. It is inherently clumsy, is capable of suggesting that, for example, establishments in the third tier were in some way inferior because of their lowly position—and that is far from being our intention—and it would moreover be rather meaningless to the general public.

125. What we should aim at must be a simple classification using everyday terms capable of acquiring a special meaning but still likely to be accepted and generally used by all concerned. We shall therefore henceforth refer to categories.

The National Museums

126. The first category is straightforward and comprises the Ulster Museum and the Ulster Folk and Transport Museum. These are generally referred to as the " national museums " and indeed the two establishments are equal in status to such institutions as the National Museum of Wales and the

Royal Scottish Museum. The fact that they are accepted as being on this level carries with it great benefits as well as obligations. They have statutory backing, are financed directly by central government and serve the whole of Northern Ireland. By and large, their staffs are appointed and remunerated on National Museum grades.

127. We find this admirable and wholly acceptable. We therefore recommend that the first category should comprise these two museums and that they should continue to be known as " national museums ". We make no comment on their operations since these are governed by statutory powers and further the subject is somewhat outside our remit. We note also that these are fully financed by central government through the Department of Education, in accordance with the statutes and subject to normal parliamentary financial control.

Regional Museums

128. We give this name to the second category, where there is most room and the greatest need for expansion. These would be fully fitted establishments so located as to make the museum experience available to the entire population of the province within relatively easy travelling distance of their homes. The specific aims which we envisage as appropriate to regional museums cannot be better stated than they are in the Department of Education and Science Report already referred to in paragraph 89, and we quote from paragraph 4.7:

" (1) to collect, safeguard and document evidence, material or otherwise, of culture, history and natural history, with appropriate emphasis on its own area;

(2) to make this evidence available to the public by appropriate means, through, for example, the provision of suitable high quality exhibition space in strategic locations and the development of museum educational services;

(3) to stimulate activities relating to these basic aims;

(4) to employ and deploy curatorial, conservation and technical expertise appropriate to the scope of the collections and services.

These are demanding specifications and their achievement will take time."

129. We had some discussion as to whether some other title than " regional " museums might be used for this category. On the whole, since their background objective must be both to mirror and to serve the region in which each is located, and since the term " regional " is already in general use, we agreed that it had best be continued.

130. This is not to say that any body or authority setting up or administering a " regional museum " must be obliged to label it as such. The word is merely a convenient label for the category and if the actual name above the

door is something else, we do not think it matters. A case in point is the regional museum in Armagh, which is still officially named the "Armagh County Museum" due to the fact that the former Armagh County Council was responsible largely for its development.

131. The Armagh County Museum is in fact the only fully operative example of a regional museum which we have in Northern Ireland. (Plate 6 illustrates a modern gallery in the Museum.) The Fermanagh County Museum in Enniskillen, operated by the Fermanagh District Council, should, if plans materialise fully, become the second regional museum. (Plate 7 reproduces a model specially constructed locally for display in the Museum.) This is still in the future, though the Council means to press ahead with enthusiasm which we applaud. We recommend that these two should be accepted as regional museums in our second category and that a number of others should be planned so as to meet the needs of the remaining areas of the province.

132. Questions now arise as to where those other regional museums should be located and, most important, how many more are really needed. We feel we must provide the right answer to these questions so that risks of over-lapping competition and ultimate wasteful duplication may be avoided.

133. Taking location first, the main criteria for choosing a place as a site for a regional museum appear to be:

1. it should be located in an area where an authority or body of some kind is prepared to be fully responsibile for its creation, ownership, upkeep and management;

2. geographically it should be in or near the main town (or one of the major towns) of its area;

3. it should be easy of access by public and private transport;

4. the area which it will serve should for reasons of history, geography, industry and/or sociology form a natural catchment area.

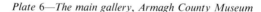

Plate 6—The main gallery, Armagh County Museum

Plate 7—Model of an Early Christian crannog or lake dwelling in the Fermanagh County Museum

134.   We have an excellent example of our thinking in this context.   The Londonderry City Council proposes to establish a museum in the city.   We have discussed their ideas with Council representatives.   We have noted that the proposal fully meets all the criteria just listed.

135.   In addition several lines for specialised treatment offer themselves:

1.   The relics of the Spanish ship *La Trinadad Valencera*, which was one of the ships of the Spanish Armada which came to grief on the north coast of Ireland, would be an ideal centrepiece of local interest.   The remains of the ship off the Co. Donegal coast have been investigated by the City of Derry Sub-Aqua Club with commendable labour and dedication.   The artefacts are now in safe custody but require extensive conservation treatment before being placed on permanent display.   There are legal complications about ownership, since the wreck-site is in the territorial waters of the Republic of Ireland, but it is to be hoped that these can be overcome so that the relics may finish up in the Londonderry Regional Museum, the obvious place for them.

2.   A second focus of interest in the whole northwest area, and one which could be an important subject for this museum, would be the narrow gauge railways of the district.   Although these operated mainly into Co. Donegal their headquarters were in the city and the lines of both the Co. Donegal Railway Co. and the Londonderry and Lough Swilly Railway Co. radiated from there.   The North West of Ireland Railway Society has valuable relics of these companies in its possession and has plans for display, including

working operations. The importance of a link between this and a section of the regional museum with the active help of the City Council is clear.

3. A third focus could be the archaeological investigations of sites recently uncovered in the city. The New University of Ulster, through Magee University College, has been and is still responsible for these. The results will in due course have great potential for the production of an authoritative exhibit displaying the history of the site upon which the city now stands and clearly research could continue under the joint auspices of the museum and the New University of Ulster.

4. A fourth focus could be on emigration from the port of Londonderry to the United States of America and to Canada, a subject with great potential interest on both sides of the Atlantic. A link could be made here with the future which we mention as possible for the Ulster-American Folk Park at Camphill (see paragraphs 221 to 224).

136. We have discussed the potential of the Londonderry Regional Museum at some length, partly in order to demonstrate how obvious it is that the city should be the site of a regional museum for the northwest of Ulster. We use these terms carefully since it seems evident to us that at least the eastern part of Co. Donegal could be regarded as being within the catchment area and we would hope that this concept would be acceptable to all the authorities concerned.

137. We also have expounded this at length partly to demonstrate how we expect a regional museum to specialise in matters appropriate to the area which it serves. Northern Ireland is rich in topics of a local or regional character where some measure of research and collection by interested people led by a professional museum curator could readily result in a regional museum being well supplied with specialist local displays. The Londonderry Regional Museum does not need to look very far to find its topics. We think that other museums would also have little difficulty.

138. The discussion just concluded about the possible nature of the Londonderry Regional Museum has a vital bearing upon the second question presently under study—how many more are really needed ? We must bear in mind the concept that regional museums should be firmly based on specialist sections reflecting the life and history of the region which they serve. If the museum is properly sited, there will be little difficulty in identifying this area although one cannot mark it off with finite lines. One area will shade into another and collaboration between the curators will therefore need to be good. We already have one example of this in the good relationship which exists between the Curators of the Armagh County Museum and the Monaghan County Museum.

139. We know that the Armagh County Museum serves an area starting roughly at the town of Newry and stretching north-westwards to merge into the area to be served by the Fermanagh County Museum. The latter in turn has a sphere of activity stretching northwards into Co. Tyrone where it

merges into the area which should be catered for by the Londonderry Regional Museum, terminating roughly to the west of Coleraine. Within these regional museum bounds there is a large area around Omagh which contains the Ulster-American Folk Park, which is discussed in our third category.

140. We consider that in this way the regional museum needs of the north-west, west and south of the province will have been met. Turning to the east we feel that the area around Belfast does not require any new provision in the regional museum category. If we draw a circle with its centre at the City Hall in Belfast and a radius of 15 miles, we include a large population all within a short journey of the national museums and we consider that their needs at regional museum level are fully met.

141. This leaves two areas, one consisting for the most part of Co. Antrim, the other largely of Co. Down. We consider that these would be amply catered for by one regional museum each, for preference sited at the optimum geographical location. So far as our criteria dictate, we are of the opinion that the one should be in or close to Ballymena, and the other in or close to Downpatrick.

142. We recommend the acceptance therefore of five locations for actual or planned regional museums—Armagh, Enniskillen, Londonderry, Bally-mena, Downpatrick; that the figure of five should be a definite target not to be exceeded; and that the aims of these museums should be those set out in paragraph 128.

143. As regards the two eastern regions we know of no proposal for the Ballymena area. In Co. Down the Down District Council is pressing on with plans for a museum in Downpatrick. Other district councils in both regions have shown active interest in the promotion of museums.

144. We do not wish to be drawn into adjudicating on rival projects nor indeed is such planning in our power. But there is this interest and in con-sequence some planning is proceeding to different degrees in each of the two areas which still lack a positive project for a regional museum. It will clearly be for central government to decide how to disburse whatever funds may become available and to say what its criteria will be. We would urge, however, that with some flexibility it should be possible for interests which look as if they may compete against each other to come together to form joint projects aimed at serving the areas and interests of all the parties. For example, several district councils might avail themselves of their statutory powers to form a consortium to provide joint finance and management.

145. It is apparent from paragraph 142 that the implementation of this policy would be likely to leave some district councils with unsatisfied ambitions for their museum projects. Examples are the Lisburn Borough Council, with a firm project in Lisburn; the Dungannon District Council with an equally firm project in Fivemiletown; the Moyle District Council with a development in Ballycastle; and the North Down Borough Council

with plans to provide museum facilities in Bangor or Holywood. We consider this should not be a contentious matter. The siting of the regional museums will leave adequate room for smaller museums in the region; these could be regarded in a way as complementary to the regional museum, since there would be great advantage if the curator of a regional museum were to act, by consent, in an advisory capacity.

146. We have not discussed the method whereby regional museums should be managed and we do not propose to go into this in detail. We see great advantage, however, in the idea of a broadly-based management committee and we recommend that the Department should adopt this as a condition for any financial assistance. The composition of the Management Committee of the Armagh County Museum, in so far as applicable, could repay study in this connection. It is most important also that a curator be appointed for the proposed museum before major development decisions are taken and that the appointment be made with the help of professional assessment.

Display Centres

147. The third category must now be described. This may be said briefly to comprise everything else coming within the definition of " museum " and not in the category of a national or regional museum.

148. Thus it could include not only those museums which have not regional status but also such widely diverse establishments as the Armagh Planetarium and the house and outbuildings at Castle Ward, or information and interpretative centres of all types at forest or country parks. The scope is wide and for the reasons given below we have found that the term " display centre " covers it best, especially since many of such establishments are not remotely like the public's idea of a museum, and may in some cases have a relatively small museum element. It is important to find some general term which can pass easily into common usage and which in the simplest words might convey some idea, however vague, of the general objective common to the whole category. The word " centre " is a good one in this connection but some of the qualifying words at present used are not attractive to us—" visitors " conveys nothing except that the place is for the use of visitors—which might mean anything; " interpretative " is clumsy and hard to understand; " educational " or " information " could be deterrent. On the whole we favour the word " display ". It is simple, wide in scope and reasonably descriptive of the content. It could equally refer to all the places we have in mind and this is the sort of bracket we must aim for. Accordingly we think the third category should consist of " display centres ", and this is our recommendation.

149. This is not a category upon which any limit of numbers can be placed. The establishments have sprung up where they are for some specific reason—the Planetarium in the grounds of the Armagh Observatory, the nature centres because they are needed at the forest or park, and the accident of natural beauty is often involved. Also the element of personal initiative

arises, since a body or person has seen a need for something and has set to and created it. We would not criticise this in any way.

150. In view of the wide scope of the term " display centre " we do not attempt to define it more closely than the description given in paragraph 147. But as with regional museums, we wish to make it clear that we do not intend that the term " display centre " should of necessity be used as a name for any individual place (though it has much to commend it). Rather it is intended to be a category label for ease of reference. Thus just as the Armagh County Museum (as stated in paragraph 130 above) is still known as such— although it would be an example of our regional museum category—so the Armagh Planetarium would be in the display centre category, but obviously would continue to use its present descriptive title.

151. One other point arises here. We have very deliberately moved away from any categorisation which would imply that establishments in one class might be considered to be better or worse than establishments in another class. For example, a display centre must in its own way be just as " good " as the national museums, by ensuring that proper professional standards are fully observed; indeed a highly specialised display centre might complement or even enlarge upon a display located in a regional or national museum. For many people the display centre will in fact have a special importance since it will not only be close to where they live but will also provide their first introduction to the interest and pleasure to be gained from visits to museums of all kinds.

152. We are anxious therefore that it should be fully appreciated that all the establishments envisaged by us are equally capable of reaching the same standards of excellence regardless of the category into which they may happen to fall. We would hope that there will not be such a thing as a " bad " museum.

IX. WHO SHOULD PROVIDE AND OPERATE MUSEUMS?

153.   One simple answer to the question posed in the title of this section is to say that any one who feels like it might do it but perhaps this is too easy a way of avoiding a difficult question.   Anyway the simple answer is not right for regional museums.   In this case we are talking of major institutions which must be firmly established, cared for and maintained in proper housing; and continuous ownership stretching indefinitely into the future must be inbuilt.   Some measure of public or corporate ownership in order to ensure this continuity would seem to impose itself.   We have no evidence of any desire to set up regional museums from any parties other than district councils and we have mentioned by name a number of these who are very actively interested.   District councils have in our view all the powers necessary and they consider that the exercise of this power would be a fitting fulfilment of their local government role.   Local authority involvement in museum ownership is of course traditional.   One need only recall the initiative of the former Belfast Corporation in setting up and developing what is now the Ulster Museum; and in Britain, outside London, local authority museums dominate the scene.

154.   In Northern Ireland we have a unique advantage in the fact that the major projects we discuss are either at a very early stage or have not yet even begun.   They can therefore be developed right from the start in accordance with strict professional museum standards.   A fundamental objective must be a balanced and coherent museum system in Northern Ireland where each element will make its contribution to the whole.

155.   The structure we recommend is designed to ensure healthy development on these lines.   We attach great importance to this and we therefore recommend that these principles must be built into government decisions resulting from our Report.

156.   It is true that for various reasons, which we need not detail, the Armagh County Museum is now by statute under the control of the Ulster Museum Trustees but is managed by a local County Museum Management Committee where a wide range of interested parties are represented.   We visited the Museum and had the benefit of a long discussion with the Chairman of the Management Committee and the Curator.   It was clear that the Museum has continued its development under the present arrangement—which dates back only to the reorganisation of local government in 1973—and that it is a strong vigorous institution, with a modern forward-looking outlook, well patronised by the local population and serving schools in the whole area of the Southern Education and Library Board, thus extending its influence into Down and Tyrone.   Its relationship with both the Education and Library Board and Armagh and neighbouring district councils is excellent.   It is thus a good example of one method of operating a regional museum.

157. This system of control of a regional museum has other advantages, such as the interchange of material and staff, some access for Armagh to the larger financial resources of the Ulster Museum, and the obvious benefits for Armagh of being able to draw directly on the Ulster Museum's technical experts.

158. We do not rule out extension of this system to new regional museums, although the existing powers of the national museums do not appear to be sufficiently wide to allow them to open branches, as it were, and it must be acknowledged that to bring about the present Armagh arrangement it was necessary to introduce amending legislation. However, there are good grounds for believing that the creation of new regional museums on this pattern would not be a sufficient fulfilment of the aspirations of district councils.

159. Mention has already been made in this Report of the present activities of a number of district councils in relation to the creation of museums. Their powers to provide and maintain museums go back as far as Section 9 of the Public Libraries Act (Ireland), 1855 and the Museums and Gymnasiums Act, 1891. These provisions together with some in other early Acts were brought up to date in 1973,* when local government reorganisation was being implemented. So it is evident that the intent of Parliament was to ensure that the newly created district councils would have the power to provide and maintain museums, and the evidence before us is that a number of district councils are anxious to exercise this power.

160. We have also strong evidence that they share a common belief that the control of new museums should rest firmly in locally constituted bodies, though they accept that linkage with a comprehensive museum structure is necessary. We gather that what they would look upon as bureaucratic interference with local management by central government is a very real threat to be avoided at all costs. We respect this view though of course we make no attempt to judge whether it is justified or not.

161. Further we note that this factor if anything strengthens the determination of those district councils to have and control their own museum. They would, however, accept joint management committees with suitable representation from other interested parties. We think this is a constructive and broad-minded approach.

162. Apart from district councils there is also the outside possibility of a regional museum being provided, owned and operated by private interests or set up with private funds. The investments throughout the United Kingdom from the Andrew Carnegie funds spring to mind, and of course the Mellon family's contribution to the Ulster-American Folk Park is our most recent example. We do not rule out this type of foundation but in this age there seems to be less of a fashion for sponsoring museums—sporting events

* The Local Government (Modifications and Repeals of Education, etc. Legislation) Order (Northern Ireland), 1973.

seem to be preferred by sponsors with money to use for public benefaction—and therefore we do not look to this source. Nevertheless, the possibility of at least material participation by, or financial assistance from, private sources or perhaps even major industrial concerns is worthy of consideration.

163. Under existing legislation we acknowledge that the new regional museums are most likely to be provided by district councils and we recommend that district councils be accepted as the most likely promoters. They may well need some financial encouragement and we shall come to this later. We accept the possibility of other bodies aspiring to promote regional museums, but we consider this to be a less hopeful direction from which to expect developments.

164. For display centres, the very width of scope of the category inevitably brings with it a complete open-mindedness on our part as to the type of body which ideally should operate such establishments and the organisation to be adopted. One can instance central departments such as Agriculture and Environment, district councils who will have a centre but not a regional museum, public bodies such as the Arts Council and the National Trust, and so on. We see no need to be specific here except to repeat that the establishments must come within our very broad definition and that there must be good cause to believe that they conform to proper museum standards, and will continue to do so.

165. We are thus in favour of a very flexible approach to display centres, with the aim of bringing serious, purposeful institutions within the compass of the museum structure. The structure will benefit from the multifarious nature of its component parts, and the parts will, we trust, contribute to each other and to the whole as well as drawing advantages to themselves Equally, display centres may expect to benefit from the regional museum service, in respect of the museum element they contain, as discussed later.

166. A highly important factor must not be lost sight of. Some display centres already in being, some others actively at the design stage, are located in places where there is already a very high annual visiting rate e.g. Tollymore Forest Park, with over 150,000 visitors annually. A high proportion of these are probably people who would not normally think of visiting a museum and indeed who would not realise that a forest park display centre can be classified as a museum. We are anxious for the museum structure to draw strength from such visitor rates so that people who may have gone to see the trees in a pleasant place may be brought to realise that there are horizons perhaps hitherto unknown to them available in museums throughout the province. The forest park display centre may be the window through which they catch the first glimpse of these wider horizons.

X. A REGIONAL MUSEUM SERVICE

167. All this will not come about of its own accord and there is one form of general service which has been discussed with us by many witnesses. This arises from the fact that display centres are being created and a great deal of enthusiasm is finding praiseworthy expression. However, standards have to be set and maintained, wasteful overlapping has to be avoided, ideas have to be shared so that they may be exploited to the full and above all authoritative advice and technical expertise must be made available. The evidence points to a strong and general feeling that guidance can come only from some central agency, and that there is a gap here which badly needs to be filled quickly.

168. We have already mentioned the valuable work done in this field by the Directors and staffs of the two national museums. They do not lightly turn away anyone who seeks their aid, nor does shortage of staff, money, or time, prevent them from lending a helping hand. But they do not have the duty to do this and their commitment to their own work leaves no room for extra loading.

169. Hence we see the need for a regional museum service. We have repeatedly referred to the necessity for all museums to aim at, to reach and to maintain proper curatorial and technical standards. Such standards are recognised within the museum profession and to achieve and maintain them requires the use of a wide range of curatorial expertise and modern display techniques—a job for specialists.

170. Trained museum personnel are, however, very scarce and anyhow it would be beyond the resources of a comparatively small display centre to employ full-time specialists in display techniques—lighting, graphics, photography, screen-printing, joinery, model-making—conservation, restoration, classification and cataloguing. Neither would the small centre be able to give full-time employment to such staff. Yet these are the skills which need to be fully exercised to create and maintain displays of the right calibre.

171. As we have just discussed we see a very clear need for the early setting up of a central organisation, and we recommend accordingly the creation of a " regional museum service ", with the following functions:

1. to be a consultant on all matters pertaining to museums;
2. to give assistance on museum problems;
3. to maintain a qualified staff for the purposes of 1 and 2 above;
4. to own and operate specialist equipment for the servicing of all museums;
5. to use the skills of experts to create and maintain the highest standards in museums.

172. There are obvious problems about the control and geographical location of the pool of expertise and tools which this proposal calls for. At present the personnel capable of being the core of this new service are nearly all to be found in the staffs of the two national museums, where they are fully employed. Both Directors have told us of approved posts lying empty for long periods because suitable candidates for them do not come forward; consequently staff are very fully employed and indeed over-employed, so that to add to their duties by widening out their responsibilities to cover all establishments within the definition of " museum " is simply not possible. Reinforcements must be found.

173. In such circumstances it would appear that at present the national museums would not be able to carry any additional work burden. As now constituted they should neither be given additional and wider responsibilities nor should they be asked to hand over staff to a new service when they are badly needed for their present duties. A regional museum service will therefore require a new organisation which will have to be able to attract extra personnel for the growing museum structure.

XI. CONTROL OF THE MUSEUM STRUCTURE AND SERVICE

174.   Such a new organisation must provide an answer to certain fundamental questions.   Who is to say which regional projects are to be approved for development and which are to be turned down?   To whom is a district council to turn for advice in drawing up its plans?   Who is to advise on any funds which may become available?   Who is to control and manage the regional museum service?   These are highly important questions to which we can see two widely differing possible answers and also a feasible midway compromise.

175.   The Department of Education advises on and implements government policy on museums, carries out central government functions in relation to the national museums and is responsible for the distribution of whatever Exchequer funds are available for museums.   If any extra finance should be made available for a new policy arising from this Report, the Department will no doubt be responsible for it also.   One answer to the questions posed in the previous paragraph is that the Department should be developed so as to be in a position to operate the regional museum service itself.

176.   The machinery necessary to do this could be devised but the fact is that the Department does not now have the staff available to deal with the sort of questions we have posed in paragraph 174 and there is no pool of museum expertise within the Department.   So the Department would have to create within itself a unit to control the regional museum service and also some means of assisting it to reach decisions on the policy matters arising. The solution might well be that of setting up a standing advisory committee together with a strengthening of departmental staff to whatever extent might be necessary.   Such an advisory committee would not require statutory backing and would be adequate to assist the Department in reaching decisions about which regional projects it should help if neighbouring promoting interests were in competition or which to reject if projected developments were too numerous or for whatever reason were to be discouraged.

177.   The Department, however, might not wish to concern itself in matters such as the day-to-day management and control of the regional museum service and indeed we are inclined to believe that this might best be left to existing specialists.   There would also be a host of small but important administrative items arising from a growing museum structure which similarly might be most easily handled by a small team of specialists.   We have in mind, as an example, a proposal by some display centre with small technical resources of its own to mount a travelling exhibition on some worthwhile subject within its own peculiar sphere of influence.   There would be decisions to be made on whether to endorse the idea, what measure of regional museum service resources to use for the project, what size and scope

to give it, which other centres to tour it around, and so on. The Department may not wish to involve itself in that sort of detail. Yet as the structure develops more and more, such questions are bound to demand answer.

178. For the Department to be put in a position to answer these questions from within, an important accession of staff would be called for. The staff necessary to operate the service would also have to be recruited and this would involve a range of personnel with curatorial and technical skills. There would also be the matter of housing, equipment etc. No doubt all this is possible but we have some hesitation about its desirability and we think that the Department could be reluctant to be involved in administration of this nature.

179. We have therefore looked at another solution which would involve the Department in the least possible degree. This would be the setting up of a statutory museum agency with the duty of administering the regional museum service. This agency could also serve as an advisory council to the Department on matters of museum policy, particularly on finance. We stress the financial point because, in the event of funds becoming available for financial assistance to museum projects, the Department would probably retain control of the funds and in evaluating proposals it might well be obliged to make unpopular decisions.

180. We envisage this as a fairly large body, with members drawn from the Trustees of the national museums and representatives of regional museums, district councils, Education and Library Boards, other major interested bodies such as the Arts Council, independent people and departmental assessors. We consider this body would have to be statutory, so that it would have power and authority to match its responsibilities. In all probability it would have to meet only from time to time to determine policy and to make major decisions.

181. We have some reluctance in proposing such a large body, especially because its size would mean that it would be cumbersome and its effectiveness could be open to doubt. Moreover it could not deal with day-to-day administration. This would have to be entrusted to an executive committee, which could meet frequently. The composition of this would probably be on the lines of the agency Chairman, the Directors of the national museums, a departmental assessor and the secretary or manager of the agency. The Secretary or Manager would clearly have to be a qualified and experienced museum professional.

182. Decisions could be made in this executive committee on a consensus basis as to, for example, the use of scarce technical resources, the interchange of exhibition material, projects involving joint research and the creation of temporary exhibitions. Above all the committee would control the deployment of the resources of the regional museum service. Under this scheme

these resources would continue to be operated as at present by the national museums. However, since the museum resources are already being used to the full, this scheme envisages that they would be augmented gradually as finance and the availability of skilled personnel permitted.

183. Whilst this type of solution might be made to work, we have to admit the possibility that it would never be very satisfactory. The national museums would continue to have first call on the services of their own staff, with the result that the calls of the regional museum service might go unanswered or at best might be dealt with only with great delays. Furthermore, the Directors acting on the executive committee could be placed in the invidious position of frequently having to make decisions in which they would be involved in assessing the needs of their own institutions against the needs of the regional museum service.

184. We do not propose to detail any further machinery such as would clearly be necessary since we conclude that a statutory advisory agency combined with the necessary executive committee is not a particularly attractive or workable solution. We thought it best, however, to devote some attention to it before rejecting it since it is the scheme most diametrically opposed to the possibility of the Department doing everything itself.

185. We now consider a third possibility of a compromise nature. This is to set up a Department of Regional Museum Services operated jointly by the Ulster Museum and the Ulster Folk and Transport Museum. This concept would entail the appointment of a joint management committee formed mainly of equal numbers from the Boards of Trustees of the national museums—perhaps three from each Board—plus one representative from each of the management committees of the five regional museums as these become effective. Whilst the committee's function would be to manage the regional museum service, it might also have some advisory functions.

186. Such a Department of Regional Museum Services would have an establishment consisting of a Keeper, an Assistant Keeper (Curatorial), an Assistant Keeper (Technical), an Education Officer, a Transport Manager, and supporting administrative and clerical staff. As the main body of the requests coming to the regional museum service is likely to be for design and display facilities we recommend that the new Department should also have a balanced team of some six specialist personnel providing a flexible service in modern design and display techniques and structures. This team would be the responsibility of the Assistant Keeper (Technical) referred to above. It also seems essential that a specialist in some aspect of conservation should be on the establishment of the new Department.

187. Thus, as envisaged, the new Department of Regional Museum Services would have at its disposal professional and technical staff who, for con-venience and expediency, should be recruited to the establishment of the Ulster Museum. Accommodation comprising offices, a design studio, a photographic darkroom, workshops, stores and garaging would need to be

Plate 8—The main picture store in the Art Department of the Ulster Museum

provided and as space is already at a premium at the Ulster Museum—and the Stranmillis site does not readily lend itself to further expansion—an obvious solution would be to locate the new development within the grounds of the Ulster Folk and Transport Museum as an additional element in the major capital development programme still to be implemented there. This we recommend. (Plate 8 illustrates the main picture store at Stranmillis and is a very good example of how space must be used to the fullest degree possible.)

188. We do not envisage that the staff of the new Department would immediately be competent in the whole range of skills which might eventually be necessary and indeed some specialist skills may well remain outside the scope of the Department. These could be contributed to it from elsewhere. However, the staffing structure outlined in the preceding paragraphs should ensure an efficient and comprehensive service capable of providing or obtaining all the skills necessary to promote a balanced and cohesive museum structure throughout Northern Ireland.

189. Being a joint Ulster Museum-Ulster Folk and Transport Museum undertaking, the new Department will be in a position to draw directly on the curatorial advice and expertise of the professional staff of these two

48

institutions, and on their collections. It is anticipated that other bodies such as the Universities, the Arts Council and the Public Record Office will be prepared to contribute by expertise in their own fields to the operation of this important new element in the overall museum structure.

190.   It is appreciated that a regional museum service on these lines will require statutory cover and this will inevitably involve some delay in the preparation of legislation and in its consideration by Parliament. We can see no alternative to this but some preparations could be made in the meantime by seeking authority for extra posts and in planning the service in detail—we have only suggested the outlines. We also appreciate the problems for the Department of seeking the funds necessary even to make a start on this programme.

191.   Nevertheless, we consider that our third possible scheme, as discussed in paragraphs 185 to 190, is the most realistic means of setting up a regional museum service and we recommend that it should be adopted.

XII. FINANCE

192. What will this cost? We were advised by the Department at the start of our deliberations that no financial provision has been made to meet the cost of any proposals we might make. This of course was inevitable since neither the nature nor the cost of these proposals could at that time be assessed. We are also not forgetful of restrictions on public spending found necessary by the government in the fight against inflation.

193. When the Department is considering our proposals, however, it must have a good idea of what they would cost to implement and we would hope that this knowledge might enable some provision to be made soon so that the foundation of the structure might be laid. We attach much importance to this, since—as we have shown—the evidence before us demonstrates that a large body of enthusiasm exists in the province in favour of museum expansion. If this is not harnessed soon, it may either wither and die, or else some elements may proceed regardless, and perhaps in a wrong direction, out of which they might later on be hard to turn. The financial implications must therefore now be weighed and considered together with any means of minimising costs so as to enable early progress to be made.

194. We look first at the cost of regional museums. Both of the existing regional museums occupy buildings of character which in themselves are worthy of preservation. The remaining three may not find themselves buildings as individual as the Keep in Enniskillen or surroundings as distinguished as the Mall at Armagh, and adaptation and fitting out of old buildings may well cost as much as new buildings. Allowing for the time taken to search, acquire, plan and implement, we see the capital cost of completing the network of five regional museums as something in the area of about £1,000,000 spread over five years from now and at 1978 price levels.

195. Must all this capital cost be borne on the public purse? We feel that it must: we commend and encourage all efforts by district councils to involve the private sector, whether by direct contribution, sponsorship, or whatever other appropriate means; but we acknowledge realities and we note the acceptance already of the principle of total public sector financial responsibility in such fields as recreation and leisure provision. While the district council will wish to retain as much control as possible of the enterprise, it should be able to call upon substantial grant from central government, and we see the Department of Education as contributing up to three-quarters of the capital cost.

196. The district council should be able to meet in full the maintenance and running costs of the regional museum, but we feel that it should be able to claim grant from the Department of Education on salaries and wages of the museum staff, especially if it is to accept direction on levels of staffing, standards of qualifications, etc. It is difficult to forecast staffing levels, but

if for the sake of an estimate an average per museum of ten staff be taken and an average salary/wage of £4,000, we see total expenditure on salaries and wages—commencing with the two existing regional museums and building up over a five-year period as the other three come in—as reaching a total annual bill of about £250,000 at full development. We feel that a grant of half this cost from the Department of Education would be appropriate.

197. We look now at the cost of the regional museum service. The existing national museums' resources will need to be supplemented, and we see this as requiring the provision of an additional building, costing perhaps £300,000 to build and fit out. We see the additional staff as costing perhaps £75,000 a year, and we see an additional £75,000 as being necessary for the considerable running costs in maintenance, materials, replacement of tools, transport and travelling, etc., which the regional museum service will entail.

198. It could be contended that the regional museum service should be supported by an annual levy on all district councils, perhaps a per capita levy. We see merit in this, but we see also the administrative labour it will cause. Besides, while the district council will be the major customer of the regional museum service it will not be its only customer. We take the view therefore that the regional museum service, being based on the national museums, should be totally financed, as they are, by central government.

199. There remains the costing of the display centre dimension. Here it is as well to bear in mind their range and diversity: display centres may be large or small, and the museum element in a display centre may be large or small. At one extreme is the district council enterprise which may closely rival a regional museum, at the other is the enterprise which is established and run for, in the main, quite different purposes but which has a small museum content. It will not be appropriate to accord to display centres grant levels as high as those for regional museums, just as it will not be appropriate to exercise the same levels of control.

200. A case could be made for not aiding capital and recurrent costs of display centres at all, especially where the activities are of mixed character. In this context we note that district councils have expressed the view that current costs should be met largely—opinions differ on the precise share—by the local authority itself, and we see merit in this. It is our strong view, however, that the museum element in a display centre can be, and should be, identified, and that it should qualify for grant from central government. We suggest fifty per cent as the level for grant aid from the Department of Education on the museum element both of capital works and of salaries and wages. The financial summaries below include a figure of £100,000 for capital development and £75,000 per annum for recurrent. It may be noted here that the summary in paragraph 202 below appears to assume that all the money to be spent on the museum element of display centres will be public money. This is an assumption deliberately made, and it appears not to acknowledge the fact that display centres will be provided by private bodies as well as public bodies. But since few such private bodies subsist

in Northern Ireland at present without a high level of public subsidy, from whatever sources, we have felt that the implications for the public purse of our financial summary are not unduly distorted by the omission of the private sector financial contribution.

201. Should the regional museum service be provided free to regional museums and display centres? We accept as a general principle that bodies making use of a service should be required to make payment for it. We are aware nonetheless of the difficulty that can arise in determining a realistic basis of charges, and we would not be disposed to object if on grounds of administrative convenience the service were to be provided free—especially since charges on all district councils and many display centres would be paid out of public funds in any case. We would maintain, however, that materials provided by the service to user bodies should be paid for, except where it suits the service to regard them as continuing to belong to it.

202. FINANCIAL SUMMARY.

CAPITAL COSTS, spread over 5 years

	Total cost to public funds £	Total Department of Education grant £
Regional museums	1,000,000	750,000
Regional museum service ..	300,000	300,000
Display centres	100,000	50,000
Totals ..	1,400,000	1,100,000

RECURRENT COSTS

Over the five-year period there will be a build up. Once all five regional museums are in operation (the display centres may of course go on developing indefinitely) the annual bills for recurrent costs will be something like this:

	Total cost to public funds £	Total Department of Education grant £
Regional museums:		
Salaries and wages ..	250,000	125,000
Other	50,000	nil
Regional museum service:		
Salaries and wages ..	75,000	75,000
Other	75,000	75,000
Display centres (museum element):		
Salaries and wages ..	50,000	25,000
Other	25,000	nil
Totals ..	525,000	300,000

We cannot end this part of the Report without drawing attention to the relatively modest cost to public funds of implementing our recommendations. At a capital cost of one and a half million pounds and an ongoing budget thereafter of some half a million pounds the province would be able to build up and service an excellent network of regional museums and display centres, sufficient to satisfy its needs for many years to come. We consider this to be a constructive and forward-looking policy and we recommend its adoption.

XIII. HOW VARIOUS ORGANISATIONS MAY FIT INTO THE MUSEUM STRUCTURE

203. In a structure such as we envisage, where flexibility must be one of the most important features, it seems inevitable that much of the detailed mechanism will grow up gradually. Hence it would be premature for us to try to foresee it all in full working order. Some consideration should be given to the way in which some of the larger existing institutions may take a place in the structure. We have in mind particularly those bodies which have a policy of their own and resources both financial and technical with the result that they are already occupants of what will be a major place in the new museum structure. We start with each in turn of the Government Departments and the various organisations for which they are responsible, or with which they are connected in some way, and which come within the ambit of our interest.

204. THE DEPARTMENT OF FINANCE is involved in two important instances—firstly, it is the source from which the NATIONAL TRUST receives some assistance for recurrent expenses. The Trust is the owner/ occupier of a large number of places coming within the widest possible interpretation of our definition of museum, including a number of outstanding houses, areas of natural beauty and wild life reserves. It is supported by members' subscriptions, entrance fees, donations and some government assistance. But the task of physically maintaining and watching over some forty establishments means that the proportion of income left for the employment of technicians and the provision of equipment for them and for display purposes is not great.

205. Yet the Trust states that its " properties are in many instances living extensions to the Museums ". This is true. The Trust also receives very large numbers of visitors at many of its establishments but it feels that these are not well enough catered for in the provision of displays and aids to understanding and interpreting what they see at the centres. So it appears that the major contribution likely to be made by the Trust to the structure is already on the ground in its forty properties. We were glad we were able to pay a visit to Castle Ward, which is a good example of a many-sided display centre with the house, the laundry, the estate buildings and the wild-fowl collection and reserve. We feel that the Trust will look to the regional museum service for assistance in technical expertise and display, as well as possibly the loan of material for purposes such as the complete furnishing of some of the houses.

206. We were much interested also in the extensive use made by school pupils of National Trust properties and the arrangements made to receive them. We thought this useful and forward-looking.

207. Secondly, the DEPARTMENT OF FINANCE is directly responsible for the PUBLIC RECORD OFFICE, which of course is the custodian of a vast quantity of material of great interest. In addition to the storage and preservation of these records, the Public Record Office is also much involved in educational work related to its collection. It already collaborates with the national museums and the National Trust on education projects and much of its work in this connection is done through the Education and Library Boards, and indeed there are arrangements for the secondment of teachers to the Public Record Office for limited periods.

208. The Public Record Office with its resources of documents would be an excellent source of material for travelling exhibitions and would, we understand, be anxious to make available its resources in an organised, disciplined manner. Whilst this may be of greater interest to the library service, documentation is nevertheless highly important in museums and the usefulness of this is obvious. The expertise of the Public Record Office in handling documents would be a contribution to the regional museum service and in turn the Public Record Office would be likely to wish to draw on the design and other skills of the regional museum service in setting up its own exhibitions.

209. From the DEPARTMENT OF AGRICULTURE, the main item is the contribution of the FOREST SERVICE, with its six forest parks—and others to come soon—as well as smaller forests, all open to the public. The Forest Service is alive to the need to extend the scope of the display centres at the forest parks and to introduce the most up-to-date display techniques as well as to introduce wider variations in the material on display. Its resources in the type of technical skill required for exhibition purposes are small and, even though the size of the operations would point to a need to strengthen the Service's own technical display resources, it will obviously wish to draw on the regional museum service for help. On the other hand the Service, with its particular expertise on forestry—a subject of increasing interest to the public—could make major contributions to displays in centres belonging to other authorities.

210. The Forest Service also has some buildings of considerable potential. We visited and saw examples at Tollymore and Castlewellan Forest Parks. We also visited a building at Castle Archdale belonging to the Department of the Environment. Such buildings when tastefully restored are most attractive in appearance and highly suitable for display purposes, besides being located in places where a high existing visitor rate can be further exploited. We were interested in the idea propounded by the Forest Service of a regional " visitor centre " in such buildings. This would be sponsored perhaps by local district councils, the Northern Ireland Tourist Board and the Forest Service, and would be a central point to which visitors would be directed and where they could obtain full information about the area, including the physical and historical background and present-day organisations and attractions, not least the regional and other museums, in fact what one might think of as a " district " museum but not competing in size or scope with the regional museums.

211. Such a project would be very suitable for advice and assistance from the regional museum service, since its usefulness in both the museum context and the visitor/tourist sphere is obvious, yet the promoting authorities would clearly need considerable technical advice.

212. The Forest Service has also an active plan to set up a Forest Service Museum at Parkanaur, Co. Tyrone. This specialised establishment would fit in well with both the biological interests of the Ulster Museum and the sociological interests of the Ulster Folk and Transport Museum and no doubt it would benefit considerably from their advice and assistance through the regional museum service.

213. The main involvement of the DEPARTMENT OF COMMERCE is through the Northern Ireland Tourist Board. Where it considers that they have an important tourist potential the Department is able to grant-aid projects approved by the Tourist Board, or to implement approved projects directly. A number of interesting projects are at present being promoted under these arrangements and most of these will result in the creation of an attraction which will come within our definition of a museum and would be classed by us as a display centre. There is an important role here for the regional museum service since its advice on setting up these places, as well as on design and layout, would be of great benefit. Examples of these are:

1. The proposed Forest Service Museum at Parkanaur;
2. The Annesley Mansions Tourist Centre at Newcastle;
3. New visitor display projects at the Giant's Causeway;
4. Dwellings, school, church, etc., connected with Patrick Brontë at Banbridge;

and some others in a less advanced stage of development.

214. Although the objective of both the Department of Commerce and the Tourist Board is to use available funds in order to enhance the province's

Plate 9—School children in the Ballyveridagh National School exhibit classroom at the Ulster Folk and Transport Museum

attractiveness to tourists—a term which can include day-trippers as well as visitors from outside the province—it is recognised by both that the main tourist business is seasonal in nature. Hence the centres encouraged by those funds will be all the more viable if there is a non-seasonal attraction.

215. We see scope here for more frequent consultation between the Departments of Education and Commerce as well as with museum authorities throughout the province with a view to ensuring that an appropriate share of the funds available to the Department of Commerce may be used in encouraging the creation of display centres. These would certainly have to be in the category of being tourist attractions but we think they should be looked upon as multi-purpose sites fitting into the general museum structure and capable of being exploited more fully because of their attractiveness to all comers. The regional museum service through its advisers would be able to assist in the planning and setting-up of the displays.

216. The bodies for which the DEPARTMENT OF EDUCATION is responsible, or which are linked with it, and which will have a part to play in the operation of the regional museum service are of great importance. Firstly, there are THE QUEEN'S UNIVERSITY OF BELFAST, THE NEW UNIVERSITY OF ULSTER, and the ULSTER COLLEGE, from all of whom we have had written evidence which by and large supports the main recommendations of this Report. Queen's University is already directly involved through, for example, its archaeological collection and the Conservation Laboratory which it operates jointly with the Ulster Museum. The New University is directly involved through ongoing work such as the wreck of *La Trinidad Valencera*, the archaeological researches on sites uncovered in Londonderry and the Guy L. Wilson Daffodil Garden. The Ulster College has shown an interest particularly in matters relating to the Arts and has made the interesting and wholly commendable point that in choosing museums " every effort should be made to utilise buildings of genuine architectural quality ".

217. Whilst these institutions might wish to draw a little upon the resources of the regional museum service, it seems more probable that their function would be to make to it contributions based upon their store of academic knowledge and experience, coupled with the services of highly specialised experts in various fields. It is evident that they are anxious to make their contribution.

218. Secondly, the views of the EDUCATION AND LIBRARY BOARDS have to a very large degree already been catered for in this Report. It should, however, be specifically mentioned that they can contribute to museums generally in various ways:

    a. by financial support for limited objectives;

    b. by assistance with premises—joint occupation by a museum and a library is an obvious possibility;

    c. by participation in management committees;

    d. by continued organisation of museum visits by schoolchildren (see plate 9);

e. generally by fostering the link between the needs of education and the provision and maintenance of museums;

f. through the contact of their libraries with a large and potentially interested section of the public.

We are in no doubt as to the great fund of goodwill in this quarter and must mention the very fruitful co-operation which exists between the boards (and under them many individual schools and libraries) and existing museums of all types. We commend the principle that museums should be an important item in school curricula, as a practical means of taking children out of the classroom environment and instilling in them in a palatable form some of the facets of the wider world around them. Museums have also an obviously important role to play in the field of continuing education.

219. Thirdly, there is the ARTS COUNCIL. Whilst much of the Council's work lies outside the field of museums, such as the promotion of music, in some important aspects there is common ground, particularly in relation to the visual arts. We have not felt it necessary during our deliberations to give any separate consideration to art galleries but they are of course included in our definition and one must remember collections such as the important and valuable holding of traditional and modern art housed in the Ulster Museum. The Arts Council, as noted elsewhere in this Report, has made an effort to bring art to the people by means of its travelling exhibitions. The expertise which it has acquired in this field will be a useful pool for the regional museum service to draw upon and arrangements should be made for this to take place, in accordance with the Council's desire to assist.

220. Regional museums and display centres would of course be visited by the touring exhibitions of the Arts Council, and the scope for collaboration here is obvious. We note that the Council has already set an example by co-operating with the Arts Council of the Republic of Ireland in promoting and travelling major exhibitions. This has been much to the benefit of all.

221. THE NORTHERN IRELAND OFFICE and THE DEPARTMENT OF THE CIVIL SERVICE have joint responsibility for the operations of the ULSTER-AMERICAN FOLK PARK, although it was initiated with funds generously donated by the Mellon family in the USA. We visited the Park on its pleasant site at Camphill, near Omagh, where have been erected a number of typical Northern Ireland buildings (some replicas, some actual reconstructions brought in from neighbouring sites) and replicas of typical 19th century American settlers' log cabins, such as were built and occupied by Ulster emigrants to North America. There is also an exhibition and information centre, café and ancillary offices. The attraction of the Park is shown by the fact that it opened as recently as 1976 but had built up attendance figures to 75,000 people—including 13,000 children in school parties—in the period July 1976 to September 1977.

222.   The Ulster-American Folk Park is unique in Northern Ireland and is likely to remain the only one of its kind here, although we have been told of plans to link it with other centres (actual or planned) connected with Ulster-American history and traditions.   Because of its specialised nature it will contribute more to the museum structure than it will ask from the regional museum service.   So far as the latter goes we would anticipate that whilst some advice from the service may at times help the Park, the latter is of such a size that it will build up its own team of skilled personnel whose assistance may well mean that the Park will play a part in the regional museum service with contributions from its own expertise.

223.   There is also the benefit to be derived from taking the opportunity of such large numbers of visitors to initiate them into the museum experience. This will happen as the Park continues to develop, especially if this is added as a specific objective in the development plans.   This aspect may be commended to the Omagh District Council, which gives active support to the Park and which might consider whether to set up a display centre of its own in or adjacent to the Park, with objectives of a wider type.

224.   We also see that the Park could fulfil a wider role by assisting other authorities, and by a general encouragement of a close study of the historical ties between Northern Ireland (and especially the north-west of the province) and North America.   Ulster emigration from the port of Londonderry may become a specialised section of the Londonderry Regional Museum whilst more academic and research aspects could with advantage be pursued by the New University.   The part to be played by the Park would be connected with interlinked studies to be made in North America and with a practical demonstration of the background to the facts emanating from exploitation of the Camphill buildings, and its primary role would be in the Ulster-American research field.

225.   THE DEPARTMENT OF THE ENVIRONMENT also comes into the museum picture in several ways.   Firstly, as the Department responsible for LOCAL GOVERNMENT, it is the link between central government and the district councils.   Beyond noting this fact, we see no need to comment.

226.   Secondly, the Department operates a growing number of COUNTRY PARKS, which are, or will be, provided with visitor centres of one type or another.   These would be classed by us as display centres and we would envisage them as customers for the regional museum service.   There is a similarity to be noted here with the centres operated in forests by the Forest Service.   There may be an element of overlapping which should be avoided and there may be some degree of pooling of resources or exhibits which should be embarked upon; these are both instances where the regional museum service would, it is hoped, make a useful and constructive contribution.

227.   Thirdly, the Department is responsible for the HISTORIC MONU-MENTS and the HISTORIC BUILDINGS COUNCILS.   The former

has a high degree of expertise in relation to the preservation and restoration of ancient buildings and ruins, and skilled staff engaged in this work; the latter has built up a store of knowledge of the stock of buildings of historic or architectural merit. The regional museum service should be able to draw upon both of these stores of knowledge.

228. We have not set out to list all the agencies which have links with central government departments but rather to highlight the more important which may well be involved in one way or another with the structure which we envisage. Similarly we are not going to comment in detail on all the other agencies, organisations and even private individuals who may be expected to make a contribution or to look for help or to find a place in the structure. There are, however, several other important examples of museum presence which remain to be discussed.

229. The first of these is the REGIMENTAL MUSEUMS. We have visited two of these and were much impressed by the quality of the exhibits and the high standard of display. The museums have a peculiarly personal significance for a great many people who have either personal military ties with the regiments concerned or who have inherited such ties from relatives—sometimes several generations back—who served in the regiments. These museums may not have much to contribute to the regional museum service. Nevertheless they must be regarded as part of the museum presence and it may well be that they should aim at some kind of linkage with the nearest regional museum. This would be appropriate since they are to a large extent a reflection of the social structure of the area from which the regiments tended to be drawn. In fact many aspects of the history of an area may be traced in the fighting career of its regiment. The museums are generally housed under one roof with the regimental office of the regiment concerned. Should amalgamation of regiments or closure of regimental offices bring up the question of the future of these museums, it would be important to retain them in the area of their regiments and not to remove them to some other and less appropriate place. The obvious way to achieve this is by the linkage we have suggested with a neighbouring regional museum.

230. We learn that in more than one instance in Great Britain an association or amalgamation of the sort indicated has been successful. A good example is the Durham Light Infantry Museum and Arts Centre in Durham whose Military Assistant has given us useful advice. In this case the Centre is administered, staffed and funded by the County Council, which has agreed to house, display and conserve the Regimental Collection, which remains the property of the Regimental Trust. The agreement works well and the Centre enjoys a high visitor rate.

231. In Enniskillen, the Fermanagh County Museum and the Royal Inniskilling Fusiliers Regimental Museum are housed in one building, the Castle Keep. In Armagh, the Royal Irish Fusiliers Regimental Museum is in a house owned by the Ministry of Defence only a hundred yards from the Armagh County Museum. In both cases good liaison already operates

and obviously a closer linkage, similar perhaps to the Durham example, could be established if necessary to save the regimental museums from being removed from their present locations, which satisfy the geographical affiliations of the regiments. Some similar solution might also be found for the other regimental museums in the province, should the need arise.

232. Convinced of the importance of these collections and the need to ensure a place for them within the museum structure, we recommend that appropriate linkages should be established or strengthened as the case may be. The regimental museums would thus be guaranteed a suitable place in the museum structure with access to the regional museum service.

233. The second example of museum presence is RAILWAY PRESER-VATION, demonstrated by bodies such as the Railway Preservation Society of Ireland and the North West of Ireland Railway Society, both of which have an immense fund of voluntary enthusiasm and a highly significant collection of railway relics, both large and small (see plate 10). The former can even claim, if it likes, to be one of the most active societies of its kind since it runs every summer a number of excursion trains in its own vintage rolling stock drawn by its own steam locomotives over the public railway system for the return trip of 120 miles from Belfast to Portrush. Steam trains and relics have a fascination all of their own, shared only perhaps by steam traction engines and vintage road vehicles. We note therefore that even in this very specialised field, the regional museum service might have a contribution to make, especially to the static displays of railway societies, and that the societies merit encouragement to ensure that their exhibitions have their place in the museum structure.

Plate 10—Disused locomotives and rolling stock of the former County Donegal Railways *at Strabane, County Tyrone, in July* 1963, *awaiting shipment to America. Some of these items are now at Victoria Road, Londonderry, with the North West of Ireland Railway Society*

234.   The third major section of organised private interest is the considerable number of LOCAL SOCIETIES specialising in history, archaeology, biology and kindred subjects.   The views held by many of these societies were conveyed to us in useful submissions by the Federation for Ulster Local Studies. Such societies have been a feature of life in Ireland for generations, sometimes coming and going as a result of the activity of one individual, sometimes lasting on through the years with a continuing strong directing committee. They may play a large part in small communities and frequently achieve the preservation of records and knowledge which would otherwise have been lost for ever.   We think that wherever possible they should be sought out and linked into a regional museum or a display centre; they are worthy of support and they have a contribution to make.

XIV. TRAVELLING EXHIBITIONS

235.   An important matter which merits brief discussion under a separate heading is travelling exhibitions.   We have referred to these several times elsewhere.   The Department of Education and Science Report already quoted from has this to say on the subject in paragraph 11.5:

" The provision of high quality travelling exhibitions is of the greatest importance in attracting to a provincial museum both the general public and local scholars.   They supplement the permanent collections and the temporary exhibitions from local resources.   In many important provincial centres the travelling exhibition is the only regular means whereby visual material, particularly in the field of the arts, can be seen in a national or international context.   This is largely a phenomenon of the period since the last war and provision was not made in the older buildings.   To take advantage of the variety of travelling exhibitions, many museums will have to make special provision, including readily adaptable accommodation which offers an adequate measure of security . . . .   Occasionally exhibits have to be stored either before or after exhibition and in very few instances are facilities adequate for the storage of objects and packing cases, and this has sometimes led to damage.   The primitive systems of heating in some galleries are potentially damaging to works of art.   An oil painting exhibition needs a strong and secure wall suspension system, with natural top lighting uncomplicated by direct sunlight.   An exhibition of water colours or textiles requires the exclusion of all natural light.   Many exhibitions need a flexible system of floor-to-ceiling space dividers for their display; all need artificial lighting which can be trained in all directions from all angles and with controlled intensity and focus; and all exhibitions of significance need a high degree of security."

236.   As we see it special attention by the regional museum service towards the fostering of travelling exhibitions within the constraints just quoted could be a useful means of paving the way for regional museums and filling a gap until such time as the museums are established.   This of course is in addition to servicing existing museums, large and small, and all kinds of places, large and small, and not necessarily display centres, where there might be a demand by the public to see the exhibition and where the necessary security for the exhibits would be forthcoming.   The regional museum service need not be the sponsor of all travelling exhibitions, far from it.   We would anticipate that every institution within the museum structure would consider whether it might at times mount a travelling exhibition centred on a topic where it has some particular qualification or expertise.   Thus the Forest Service might well contribute touring exhibitions based on its own subject, the growing of trees in Northern Ireland.

237.   There have been most commendable initiatives in this field already, the most significant being that of the Arts Council.   The Council has usually at least two highly professional exhibitions touring the province at any one

63

time and is expert not only at choosing a subject and mounting the exhibition but also at seeking out and using whatever suitable premises it can find. Thus in the early part of 1978 the travelling exhibition "Realism Now" was in Armagh County Museum from 13 to 24 February and then it moved on to spend 27 February to 10 March at the Castlereagh Swimming Baths. The second one "New Paintings" spent 6 to 17 March in Downpatrick Cathedral and then moved on to the Ulster College for the period 3 to 14 April.

238. The Armagh County Museum has recently toured an exhibition of railway relics to various places in Northern Ireland, some quite far from Armagh, and the Arts Council has toured right round the province one which originated from the Fermanagh County Museum, called "Images of Stone", based on the White Island figures (see plate 11).

239. So the regional museum service would have a good foundation to build on, using existing knowledge and experience. There would be the mechanics of selection, setting up, transport, security and so on to be worked out, and this is not a task for us. Sufficient to say that we see this as a highly important development area. We recommend that the regional museum service should be charged with the duty of fostering travelling exhibitions and provided with the means of helping to set them up. We do not mean that the initiative in creating a travelling exhibition should come from the regional museum service—though it could do so—but rather that the creating authority should come to the regional museum service to seek its guidance

Plate 11—Images of Stone, *an Arts Council travelling exhibition, based on the White Island figures, County Fermanagh, at the Shambles, Hillsborough*

and help. The regional museum service might also produce an annual programme of travelling exhibitions to ensure that facilities were used to the full but that there would not be overcrowding of the area at any time.

240. Travelling exhibitions need not of course be confined to a watertight compartment bounded by the Northern Ireland museum structure. We would like to think that exhibitions initiated outside Northern Ireland would continue to visit the province and that they would visit more centres here and be seen by more people as a result of the growth of our museum structure. Such travelling is of course expensive in money and museum resources. We note that the Victoria and Albert Museum has felt obliged to discontinue a service of this nature from which the province has benefited in the past. We feel that this is a serious loss and we would hope that if economic circumstances would ease there could be a growth of exchange of single major items, displays and exhibitions, not only within the British Isles but perhaps even in the context of the European Economic Community.

241. The prospect of EEC involvement may seem of the nature of a pipe-dream but sharing of cultural resources lies within the objectives of the Community. As their policy develops some benefit might come to our museums, whether under their cultural heading or else in the context of EEC Regional Aid Schemes. We would hope to contribute in our turn to the Community. A travelling exhibition from Northern Ireland might even make an interesting impact on continental centres. This is an example of the kind of plan which might be initiated and sponsored by the regional museum service once it is in operation and always provided that resources could be found to finance it.

XV. OTHER MATTERS

242. Several other points are left which require to be considered briefly since they arise directly from the general consideration. There is the LEGAL POSITION to which we have already made reference, and on which we have had advice from the Department of Education. We cannot of course give any interpretation of the law. Nevertheless we can give our view, as we have mentioned already, that district councils are fully empowered to provide, own and operate museums; the law is therefore no obstacle to our proposal that they may be the providers of regional museums and, where they desire, display centres. Other bodies such as the National Trust, the Arts Council, the Tourist Board have already in one way or another adequate cover for their activities.

243. On the other hand a regional museum service is not specifically provided for in any legislation. We think also that it is doubtful whether the very specific legislation relating to the two national museums* envisages the operation by them of a regional museum service. Legislation for this purpose would seem to be essential.

244. We consider that there is always benefit from having specific purposes covered by specific legislation, and indeed such is usually taken to be the will of Parliament. If the idea of a statutory body to operate the regional museum service were to be accepted, or if a regional museum service is to be set up under the compromise solution, legislation will, it seems, be necessary. Whatever decision the Department of Education reaches on our proposals, we recommend therefore that its resultant policy should be the subject of an enabling Bill so that, if Parliament approves, the Department might thereafter implement its museums policy as and when financial and other considerations would permit.

245. There is also the highly important area of MUSEUMS PUBLICITY. Each institution in the structure must be responsible for producing its own guides to its exhibition and also its own publicity material, as well as items such as art reproductions or souvenir postcards for sale to the visiting public. The introduction of a museum structure with a regional museum service means that something else becomes necessary—an overall publicity policy with two objectives: to list and describe in a single document all the members of the structure and to obtain joint publicity for them. We recommend that the regional museum service should be given the duty to look after these matters, and that in doing so they seek the aid of the Northern Ireland Tourist Board, in order to supply publicity material to visitors and tourists, and of newspapers and the broadcasting and TV authorities as appropriate, in order to place the museum picture well and truly before the home market.

* The Museum Acts (Northern Ireland), 1961 to 1973 and the Ulster Folk and Transport Museum Acts (Northern Ireland), 1958 to 1973.

246.   In the area of publicity there is also the question of attracting people to museums by special efforts which need not be themselves of a museum nature.   We have in mind events such as the wide-ranging programme of musical and other events organised by the Ulster Museum.   We are also thinking of the lectures on all sorts of topics which both national museums can cater for because they have the necessary equipment and accommodation.   Any efforts of this nature which result in bringing people into museums are worthwhile.   This emphasises the point that museum buildings should aim always at having space to spare which can be used not only for travelling exhibitions, but also for music, lectures and displays of public interest.

XVI. SUMMARY OF RECOMMENDATIONS

1. The term " museum " should be broadly defined, in accordance with the International Council of Museums' definition—paragraph 86.

2. The aims of museums can be summarised as collection, communication and research—paragraph 88.

3. The objectives which museums should have—paragraph 89.

4. Museum authorities should have amongst their major objectives a reflection of the local scene—paragraph 92.

5. A future museum structure should include a museum service—paragraph 99.

6. A central policy for staff needs is required—paragraph 102.

7. A positive forward-looking policy towards the creation of regional museums and a regional museum service is necessary on the part of central government—paragraph 105.

8. Museums should be encouraged as one of the most tangible ways of harnessing the growing public awareness of a need to conserve the best in the province's traditions and surroundings—paragraph 119.

9. A new museum structure is necessary—paragraph 120.

10. For the purposes of determining a policy museums should be divided into three categories—national museums, regional museums, and display centres—paragraphs 121, 122 and 125.

11. " National museums " should comprise the Ulster Museum and the Ulster Folk and Transport Museum—paragraph 127.

12. The aims of regional museums should be collection, conservation, documentation and presentation of material, with appropriate emphasis on their own areas—paragraph 128.

13. The word " regional " need not appear in the actual name of a regional museum—paragraph 130.

14. Armagh County Museum and Fermanagh County Museum should be accepted as regional museums—paragraph 131.

15. The criteria for the location of a regional museum should be those detailed in paragraph 133.

16. New regional museums should be located in Londonderry and in or close to Ballymena and Downpatrick—paragraphs 134 and 141.

17. There should be no more than five regional museums—paragraph 142.

18. Regional museums should have broadly-based management committees—paragraph 146.

19. " Display centres " should comprise those facilities included in the definition of " museum " which are not national or regional museums—paragraph 147.

20. No limit should be placed on the number of display centres—paragraph 149.

21. Display centres need not be known as such—paragraph 150.

22. Institutions in one museum category should not be considered to be better or worse than those in another category. All should be capable of reaching the same standards of excellence—paragraphs 151 and 152.

23. District councils should be accepted as the most likely promoters of regional museums—paragraphs 153 and 163.

24. A balanced and coherent museum system, developed in accordance with strict museum standards, should be a fundamental objective of government policy—paragraphs 154 and 155.

25. Display centres should continue to be provided and operated by a wide variety of bodies—paragraph 164.

26. A regional museum service should be established with specified functions —paragraphs 169 and 171.

27. The operation of the regional museum service by the Department of Education, with a non-statutory committee to advise the Department on policy matters, would not be the best arrangement—paragraphs 175-178.

28. The operation of the regional museum service under a broadly-based statutory museum agency, with an executive committee for day-to-day administration, would be a possible but cumbersome arrangement— paragraphs 179-184.

29. The regional museum service should be formed by the establishment of a Department of Regional Museum Services operated jointly by the Ulster Museum and the Ulster Folk and Transport Museum—paragraph 185.

30. This Department should be managed by a joint management committee —paragraph 185.

31. The staffing of the Department of Regional Museum Services should be as detailed in paragraph 186.

32. While the Department should be located at the Ulster Folk and Transport Museum site, staff should be recruited to the establishment of the Ulster Museum—paragraph 187.

33. The level of Department of Education grant on regional museum capital costs should be up to 75%—paragraphs 194 and 195.

34. The level of Department of Education grant on regional museum recurrent costs should be 50% (salaries and wages only)—paragraph 196.

35. The capital and recurrent costs of the regional museum service should be met entirely by the Department of Education. A levy should not be made on district councils—paragraphs 197 and 198.

36. The level of Department of Education grant on the museum element of display centre costs should be 50% of capital costs and 50% of recurrent (salaries and wages only)—paragraphs 199 and 200.

37. The services provided by the regional museum service to regional museums and display centres should be free of charge except as regards materials used—paragraph 201.

38. A policy of museum development on the lines suggested would meet the province's needs well and should be adopted by government—paragraph 202.

39. The regional museum service should foster travelling exhibitions although it need not be the sponsor of all travelling exhibitions—paragraph 236.

40. The regional museum service should develop travelling exhibitions using the knowledge and experience of bodies such as the Arts Council—paragraph 239.

41. The regional museum service should produce an annual programme of travelling exhibitions and should ensure that facilities in an area are well provided for but that the area is not overcrowded—paragraph 239.

42. The possibility of Northern Ireland exhibitions travelling outside the province and exhibitions visiting the province from outside should be considered. The EEC museum dimension should be borne in mind—paragraphs 240 and 241.

43. Legislation should be introduced specifically to provide for a regional museum service—paragraphs 243 and 244.

44. The regional museum service, with assistance from the Northern Ireland Tourist Board, should provide publicity for the museum structure as a whole—paragraph 245.

45. Special events of both a museum and non-museum nature should be held in museums to attract the public to them—paragraph 246.

APPENDIX A

BODIES AND INDIVIDUALS WHO SUBMITTED EVIDENCE TO THE WORKING PARTY

Arts Council of Northern Ireland
Association of Local Authorities of Northern Ireland
Association of Northern Ireland Education and Library Boards
Carrickfergus Borough Council
City of Derry Sub-Aqua Club
Combined Irish Cavalry Museum
Confederation of British Industry (Northern Ireland Office)
Department of Agriculture
Department of Commerce
Department of the Environment
Down District Council
Dungannon District Council
Fermanagh District Council*
Fisheries Conservancy Board for Northern Ireland
Foyle Fisheries Commission
Hillsborough and District Committee
Londonderry City Council**
Moyle District Council†
Newry and Mourne District Council
North Down Borough Council
Northern Ireland Chamber of Trade
Northern Ireland Council of Social Service
Northern Ireland Tourist Board
North-West Council of Social Service
North West of Ireland Railway Society
Omagh District Council
Pigs Marketing Board (Northern Ireland)
Police Authority for Northern Ireland
Public Record Office of Northern Ireland
Railway Preservation Society of Ireland
Seed Potato Marketing Board for Northern Ireland
Southern Education and Library Board
Strabane District Council
The Federation for Ulster Local Studies
The Historic Buildings Council
The Historic Monuments Council

* Meeting with the Arts and Museum Committee and the Arts Advisory Committee of the Council.
** Meeting with the Amenities and Leisure Committee of the Council.
† Submission from officers of the Council.

The National Trust
The New University of Ulster
The Northern Ireland Chamber of Commerce and Industry
The Planetarium, Armagh
The Queen's University of Belfast
The Right Honourable the Lord O'Neill of Antrim
The Royal Irish Fusiliers Regimental Museum
The Royal Ulster Rifles Museum
The Young Farmers' Clubs of Ulster
Ulster-American Folk Park
Ulster College
Ulster Farmers' Union
Ulster Folk and Transport Museum*
Ulster Museum*

* A joint Ulster Museum—Ulster Folk and Transport Museum submission.

APPENDIX B

BODIES WHOSE REPRESENTATIVES SUBMITTED SUPPLEMENTARY ORAL EVIDENCE TO THE WORKING PARTY

Armagh County Museum (Ulster Museum)
Arts Council of Northern Ireland
Department of Agriculture
Department of Commerce
Department of the Environment
Northern Ireland Tourist Board
Public Record Office of Northern Ireland
The Federation for Ulster Local Studies
The National Trust
The Royal Irish Fusiliers Regimental Museum
Ulster-American Folk Park

APPENDIX C

ATTENDANCE FIGURES FOR MUSEUMS AND ANALOGOUS FACILITIES 1972-1977

1. Ulster Museum

1972	1973	1974	1975	1976	1977
185,172	188,772	210,483	193,456	187,441	189,383

2. Ulster Folk and Transport Museum

	1972	1973	1974	1975	1976	1977
Folk Museum, Cultra	52,437	63,473	60,635	92,057	90,148†	80,546†
Transport Museum—						
(a) Witham Street, Belfast	11,802	10,446	10,590	14,232	9,777	9,042
(b) New Galleries, Cultra	—	—	—	—	49,397*†	64,233†
Total	64,239	73,919	71,225	106,289	149,322	153,821

* The new galleries were opened in May 1976.
† The figure for a particular section of the Museum merely indicates the number of visitors who entered the Museum by that section. Tickets are valid for both the folk and transport sections of the Museum.

3. Armagh County Museum

1972	1973	1974	1975	1976	1977
11,761	11,546	11,189	15,138	15,400	13,012

4. Fermanagh County Museum and the Royal Inniskilling Fusiliers Regimental Museum

1977
8,500*

* Fermanagh County Museum was not opened until April and then only for temporary exhibitions and limited periods. The Royal Inniskilling Fusiliers Regimental Museum was open throughout the year.

5. The Royal Irish Fusiliers Regimental Museum*

1972	1973	1974	1975	1976†	1977
850	920	880	720	610	780

* The above figures record only those visitors who signed the visitors' book.
† The Museum was closed for five weeks in May and June of 1976.

6. Ulster-American Folk Park

July 1976-September 1977 (inclusive)
75,000

7. The National Trust

	1972	1973	1974	1975	1976	1977
Ardress	2,063	1,016	833	1,275	731	1,067
Castle Ward	21,012	22,709	21,488	26,251	33,306	26,814
Castle Coole	3,065	2,867	2,162	3,374	3,503	3,074
Derrymore	779	Closed owing to terrorist damage				
Florence Court	1,192	2,168	1,414	2,106	2,069	2,488
Mount Stewart	6,829	9,043	8,964	9,694	13,134	24,741
Mussenden Temple	4,122	3,826	4,395	5,413	No record:admission fee removed	
Rowallane	12,826	10,796	10,224	12,605	13,507	10,928
Springhill	2,545	3,857	3,109	3,856	3,093	3,758
Temple of the Winds	1,266	4,218	2,737	3,802	3,392	4,419
Wellbrook Beetling Mill	1,357	1,890	1,354	1,069	858	1,402
Total	57,056	62,390	56,680	69,445	73,593	78,691

Estimated visitor figures for some National Trust open space properties in 1977

Giant's Causeway	150,000
Murlough Nature Reserve	100,000
Mourne Coastal Path and Bloody Bridge Path	50,000
Downhill	20,000
Carrick-a-Rede	15,000
Kearney	10,000
Fair Head and Murlough Bay	10,000

8. Forest Parks*

	1972/73	1973/74	1974/75	1975/76	1976/77	1977 (April to December)
Castlewellan	87,000	100,000	87,000	79,000	96,000	65,000
Drum Manor	10,000	18,500	25,000	27,000	28,000	24,000
Glenariff†	25,500	23,000	18,000	21,000	23,000	54,500
Gortin Glen	31,000	38,000	38,000	33,500	47,000	39,000
Gosford	18,500	15,500	20,000	24,000	28,000	24,000
Tollymore	111,000	128,500	131,000	157,000	160,000	113,500
Total	283,000	323,500	319,000	341,500	382,000	320,000 (9 mths. only)

* Figures are for financial years—1 April to 31 March.
† Glenariff did not open as a forest park until 1 April, 1977.

9. The Planetarium

1972	1973	1974	1975	1976	1977
11,000	13,000	18,000	20.000	22,000	22,000*

* July to December only. The Planetarium was closed for repairs from January to June.

APPENDIX D

ARTS COUNCIL TRAVELLING EXHIBITIONS
ATTENDANCE FIGURES 1972-77

Note: No records of attendances were kept where exhibitions were in an open area.

1972

Ulster Places

Centre	Dates	Attendances
Ballymena	31 January-11 February	1,073
Antrim	1-6 April	872
Coleraine	11-20 April	431
Craigavon	2-11 May	251
Cookstown	16-25 May	236
Ballymoney	30 May-6 June	662

Arts Council Collection

Centre	Dates	Attendances
Armagh	6-25 March	586
Armagh	3-21 April	940

Ulster Faces

Centre	Dates	Attendances
Ballymoney	28 November-7 December	464
Armagh	12-21 December	510

1973

Ulster Faces

Centre	Dates	Attendances
Newtownards	2-11 January	757
Craigavon	30 January-8 February	540
Enniskillen	12-22 February	590
Coleraine	13-22 March	864
Downpatrick	2-6 April	495
Ballymena	9-19 April	864
Antrim	21 May-31 May	no record

Arts Council Collection
Bridle/Scott/Flanagan

Centre	Dates	Attendances
Enniskillen	13-22 February	no record

Tutankhamun

Centre	Dates	Attendances
Armagh	23 October-1 November	721
Antrim	6-15 November	no record
Downpatrick	20-29 November	659
Ballymoney	4-14 December	567

1974

Tutankhamun

Centre	Dates	Attendances
Newtownards	15-24 February	331
Coleraine	19-28 March	354

Collection of An Chomhairle Ealaion

Centre	Dates	Attendances
Armagh	12 February-2 March	763
Enniskillen	28 June-5 July	no record

Drawings

Centre	Dates	Attendances
Armagh	24 September-3 October	587
Coleraine	8-18 October	396
Omagh	22-31 October	878
Newtownards	6-14 November	406
Newry	19-28 November	651
Holywood	3-13 December	223

Art in Context

Centre	Dates	Attendances
Enniskillen	14-25 October	156
Armagh	5-14 November	384
Bangor	26 November-5 December	217

1975

Drawings

Centre	Dates	Attendances
Cookstown	21-30 January	167
Enniskillen	18-27 February	360
Magherafelt		
Mid-Ulster Hospital	4-13 March	no record
Downpatrick	18-27 March	314
Ballymoney	5-24 April	824
Bangor	6-15 May	276
Ballymena	20-29 May	347
Antrim Forum	3-12 June	no record
Carrickfergus	17-26 June	481

Art in Context

Centre	Dates	Attendances
Newtownards	27-31 January	159
Antrim Forum	11-20 March	no record
Ballymoney	15-24 April	824
Cookstown	29 April-8 May	164
Newry	13-22 May	198
Coleraine	4-12 June	279

Women of Ulster

Centre	Dates	Attendances
Hillsborough	1-11 October	518
Armagh County Museum	21 October-7 November	656
Bangor	11-20 November	355
Antrim Forum	25 November-4 December	no record

1976

Women of Ulster

Centre	Dates	Attendances
Carrickfergus	5-9 January	384
Ballymena	13-22 January	300
Larne	26-30 January	303
Newry	2-6 February	1,335
Warrenpoint	9-13 February	342
Banbridge	1-5 March	215
Cookstown	8-12 March	249
Downpatrick	16-25 March	1,123
Ballycastle Town Hall	5-9 April	no record
Ballymoney Town Hall	12-16 April	348
Castlereagh Swimming Pool	20-28 April	no record
Newtownards Town Hall	11-20 May	289
Austins, Londonderry	25 May-3 June	no record
Lurgan Library	7-11 June	no record
Tourist Office, Enniskillen	15-29 June	no record
Portrush Town Hall	6-15 July	560

An Introduction to Ulster Architecture

Centre	Dates	Attendances
Antrim Forum	6-15 January	no record
Strabane	20-29 January	355
Newtownards	3-12 February	347
Ballycastle	16-20 February	496
Armagh	24 February-12 March	488
Bangor	15-25 March	247
Tourist Office, Enniskillen	17-22 May	no record
Carrickfergus Town Hall	30 June-9 July	372

Illustrations of the Eighteen Sixties

Centre	Dates	Attendances
Ballymoney Town Hall	14-23 September	423
Newtownards Library	28 September-7 October	no record
Melvin Hall, Strabane	12-21 October	437
Limavady Town Hall	26 October-2 November	367
Magee Room		
Town Hall, Larne	23 November-2 December	514
Banbridge Library	7-16 December	no record

Images of Stone

Centre	Dates	Attendances
Omagh Library	19 October-4 November	no record
Antrim Forum	9-25 November	no record
Technical College, Newry	30 November-9 December	no record
Armagh County Museum	14-30 December	413

1977

Illustrations of the Eighteen Sixties

Centre	Dates	Attendances
Teachers' Centre, Rathvarna, Lisburn	11-20 January	442
Armagh County Museum	25 January-5 February	369
Teachers' Centre, Seacourt, Bangor	8-17 February	464
Rathfriland Library	22 February-3 March	no record
Antrim Forum	8-17 March	no record
Glengormley Library	22-31 March	no record
Lurgan Library	5-14 April	no record
Cookstown Town Hall	19-28 April	348
Ballycastle Museum	3-12 May	457
Carrickfergus Town Hall	17-26 May	433
Coleraine Town Hall	31 May-9 June	392

Images of Stone

Centre	Dates	Attendances
Swimming Pool, Castlereagh	4-13 January	no record
Ballymoney Town Hall	18-27 January	474
Newtownards Library	1-10 February	no record
Limavady Town Hall	15-24 February	349
Melvin Hall, Strabane	1-10 March	387
Down Cathedral, Downpatrick	15-24 March	654
Fermanagh County Museum	12-21 April	689
Larne Town Hall	26 April-5 May	346
Brownlow Teachers' Centre, Craigavon	10-20 May	no record
The Shambles, Hillsborough	24 May-3 June	480